MW01295140

An Italian Village
a Perspective on Life Beside Lake Como

Paul Wright

Copyright © 2018 Paul Wright

Text illustrations Copyright © 2018 Paul Wright

All rights reserved.

ISBN: 9781980566465

www.sheerdesignandtypesetting.com
Cover design by Earlswood Press
Cover illustration by Paul Wright
info@wrightart.com
www.wrightart.com

To my daughter, Sammie
and to my cats,
Stevie G, Luis, Nando, Crewe Alexander, and Ulisse

CONTENTS

Also by Paul Wright

The first book of the Italian Trilogy is
An Italian Home - Settling by Lake Como

The third book is
**Cats do eat Spaghetti –
Living with our Rescue Cats**

About the Author

Paul Wright is an award-winning artist who specialises in murals, Trompe l'Oeil painted furniture, contemporary oil paintings and watercolour landscapes of Lake Como.

In 1982, following a period spent designing theatre, TV and film sets around the UK, Paul started his own art studio in Surrey, where he specialised in hand painted interiors for private homes and commercial premises.

In 1991, he moved to northern Italy with his wife Nicola, where he continues to work from his studio and art gallery base in the beautiful medieval village of Argegno on the shores of Lake Como, and from where he travels to other European countries and to the USA.

Paul's work has been featured in many art exhibitions and on two live interview programmes for Italian television, plus dozens of periodicals and newspapers worldwide, notably *The Sunday Times, Architectural Digest, The Wall Street Journal* and *The Arts Review*.

1 Swapping Villages

Towards the end of 1990, we were set to move from our Elizabethan cottage in the southern market town of Godalming in Surrey, England, to the ancient village of Arcos de la Frontera in Andalusia southern Spain. Then, my partner Nicola decided to telephone her friend, Elaine Masin, who lived with her family in a medieval village on the shores of Lake Como in northern Italy, to inform her that we were considering emigrating. Within twenty minutes of Nicola's phone call, and somewhat to my amazement, our plans had been completely changed. After twenty years of living by the Lake, Elaine's Venetian husband had been transferred to Rome for work and they needed to rent out their house.

I was, and still am a professional artist, specialising in large scale mural painting, watercolours and Trompe l'Oeil l'oeil hand painted furniture. Before that, I spent eighteen years as a stage designer and scenic artist, in repertory theatres, London's West End, for the BBC at the Television Centre in Wood Lane, for TV commercial companies and various British film studios. Prior to that, following three years at Southport Art College I painted murals on the interiors in some of Liverpool's beat clubs during the "Mersey Sound" era of the 1960s, as well as playing soccer on Merseyside at a semi-professional level.

When I first met Nicola, she was working as a surveyor's assistant in Godalming, but after five years she changed career and become a legal secretary for a local firm of solicitors. I had grown increasingly despondent about life in England, and one day I asked Nicola how she felt about emigrating to Spain. I felt that moving abroad would be beneficial for us, because the customary ten year boom and bust cycle was in full swing once more and Britain had gone into a financial downturn. Whenever there are problems with the economy, art commissions, like anything else that isn't essential to the well-to-do householder are put on hold. Commissions for my work had become very thin on the ground and I didn't want to hang around waiting for an upturn in the economy.

Nicola, on the other hand wasn't feeling the pinch. Her job was handling both divorce and property conveyancing, and at that time divorce statistics were going through the roof. Also, I made my suggestion about emigrating just after the Christmas and New Year holiday period, when couples are most likely to embark on a divorce. Nevertheless, I knew that deep down she was thrilled at the prospect of living abroad. Like me, she was fond of Spain, but she was hesitant about moving because she wasn't convinced it was feasible. It was only after her telephone call to Elaine that she became enthusiastic, because together they decided that she and I were going to rent the Masins' house for a year. They had decided upon a period of a year, because Elaine couldn't be sure their move to Rome would work for them. Equally, Nicola couldn't be certain that our move to Italy would work for us.

There was another reason for Nicola choosing Italy rather than Spain. Fifteen years earlier, when she was seventeen, she'd been an au pair for Elaine's family and because of that she could speak Italian fairly fluently. I knew the area around Lake Como too, because we had visited the Masins five years before and really enjoyed our time there. A further reason for Nicola's decision was that Elaine had contacts in the Como area who might be able to help us find work. On the other hand, neither of us could speak Spanish and we had no contacts living there. A week later, Nicola handed in the three months' notice her company required of her and a month after that, on April 9 1991, we arrived in the village of Moltrasio. It proved to be a red-letter day in our lives.

~ ~ ~

Some people say it takes great courage to swap countries, especially starting afresh in a non-English speaking one, but we were looking forward to the challenge. Because we had visited Italy on other occasions, we felt that everything about the country would be worth the effort. We left with no strings attached and arrived as straight and possibly naïve foreigners, with no assurances, no guarantees and no jobs lined up. We took a chance and trusted in luck. The only thing we had to fall back on was that if we failed to stay the course, we still owned our house in Godalming. We arrived in Moltrasio with ten thousand pounds and we estimated that if we were careful and if we didn't find any work, we could make it last for a year. My philosophy was that if it didn't work out, at least we could be certain of some sunshine during the summer months. If nothing else, we were long overdue suntans!

Looking back, after residing in the country for the past twenty-seven years, with hardly a day spent out of it except for the occasional working trip or to attend weddings and funerals in the UK, we still believe the move was the best thing we ever did. However, it wasn't always milk and honey and at times it was a case of digging in, especially in the early days and particularly for me when I was trying to learn the language at the same time as getting used to a very different mind-set and culture.

We also had to climb a mountain of almost limitless Italian bureaucracy; the difficult encounters at Como police station over an unfathomable plethora of documentation the authorities demanded before they would issue us "foreigners" (even though we were EU citizens) with a *permesso di soggiorno per stranieri* (permit of stay for foreigners) will never be forgotten. From these experiences we thought it was obvious that the Italian state doesn't want foreigners working in Italy. It was as if the government had formulated what is to all intents and purposes an admission examination: the ones who manage to pass it prove they are serious about staying and will have earned the right to stay. With millions of its own people out of work, Italy doesn't need foreigners, EU citizens or otherwise, knocking on its door, making the situation even worse. Therefore the system is intentionally made as hard as possible to comprehend. We eventually received the permesso, because without this vital document it is impossible for the foreigner to find legitimate work or operate a business properly. Slowly but surely, after applying for further documentation essential for survival in Italy we learnt how to live permanently, thereby allowing us to relish the atmosphere, the outstanding food and wines, the stunning scenery and exceptional people.

One of our principal reasons for moving south was to savour all aspects of life in an ancient Mediterranean village. We wanted to get back to a lifestyle that used to exist in the UK when it had an identity and continuity. We wanted to be in a place where we would wake up in the morning and it would be the same as it had been the day before: with no unnecessary changes and in harmony amongst a group of people who had the same values that we had.

To be part of the annual village Carnival, when I designed and painted the float, and in which Nicola took part was exciting. Learning to dance so we could join in traditional festa celebrations was good fun. The all-day eating and drinking coach trips to other parts of Italy that cost next to nothing were, and continue to be outstanding. Watching the annual *palio*, the village sports competition take place in summer temperatures and my playing football for Moltrasio in soccer tournaments was exhilarating. Being involved in the Christmas nativity scene was fascinating, then being invited to join in fantastic Christmas and New Year celebrations with some of the warmest people in Europe was a true privilege.

Without doubt the rewards for making the effort to immerse ourselves in the local culture far outstripped the downsides and we turned from flirting with the idea of living in Italy to falling in love with it; so much so, we dislike having to leave the country even for brief moments and we have never once contemplated either returning to the UK or living elsewhere in the world.

My sunbathing activity only lasted for six weeks, because Elaine's contacts pointed me in the right direction for finding plenty of work. In the end, we stayed in the Masins' house for three years and it might have been possible to stay longer, except they needed to sell the house to raise the money to put their two children through university. After that, we moved into an apartment in the historical part of Moltrasio, above a disused, three-hundred-year-old butchers shop. I subsequently rented the shop, which I converted into a much-needed art studio. We had not moved earlier because we were still unsure that our adventure would work for us. Also, we were apprehensive about committing ourselves to a rental contract with a landlord we didn't know, but the need to move gave us the shove we needed.

For a further eight years everything went fine. Nicola was working in Milan for a PR company. I received a number of art commissions to paint murals in the homes of some wealthy clients, and from my studio I sold both watercolours of the region and my unique, hand painted Trompe l'Oeil furniture to passing tourists. Then, suddenly we were shaken out of our comfort zone by a series of significant events. The first one happened on the morning of September 11 2001, when an Al Qaeda faction destroyed the World Trade Centre in New York City. A few days later, Al Qaeda's leader, Osama bin Laden issued the prophetic words, 'The world will never be the same place again.' The repercussions of that atrocity didn't do my business or anybody else's any good, as tourists fled Italy on the first available plane.

Five months after that, on January 1 2002 the second blow hit, when euro was launched. It affected everybody in mainland Europe, and finished off any hope that the slump in the tourist trade caused by the September 11 atrocity was only temporary. Practically overnight, the price of a holiday rose by twenty-five per cent, in line with the rise in the cost of living in the Euro zone. That spring, when the holiday season was supposed to be starting, the few foreign visitors who did visit my studio all remarked on how expensive they found Italy compared to their previous visit when the lira was the currency.

The third reason was much closer to home and it happened on the evening of the eighth anniversary of our living in the apartment. Three months after the advent of the Euro, a hand-delivered letter dropped onto the doormat, informing us that the rent on our flat would be increased by twenty-five per cent, with immediate effect. As if this wasn't bad enough, a month later another letter arrived, demanding a separate rent rise of thirty per cent for my art studio. My immediate reaction was to confront our landlady over these considerable increases, but after further consideration, we decided to direct our energies into moving house.

On asking around, it appeared that rents were being hiked up all over the local area. Likewise, thanks to the euro property prices were escalating beyond reason, so rather than waste time squabbling over the rent of our flat or waste time hunting for something with a rent we could afford, buying a place of our own became our immediate goal before we were priced out of that market too. Unfortunately we were in for another shock. After viewing only three properties for sale, we discovered we already had been priced out of Moltrasio, which had suddenly become the twelfth wealthiest community in the whole of Italy. For such a tiny village to hold its own with the big cities was a dubious accolade, but we could not hang around to appreciate it before it became number eleven.

Until the moment our rents were increased, we had not seriously considered buying a property, but after we had made the decision to buy, we knew that unless we won the national lottery we would have to look further afield. Seven years previously we had sold our Elizabethan cottage in Godalming but had been hesitant about entering the housing market in Italy, as offshore investment rates had been satisfactory. But following the slump, the stock market boom of the early 2000s, the drop in interest rates and the uncertainty of the world economy, people had returned to buying bricks and mortar as a secure investment and we were being left behind. Suddenly we found ourselves trying to compete against an influx of highly paid Italian and international soccer stars, both past and present, as well as business tycoons, oligarchs, property developers and what can be called the "celebrity effect" with the likes of film star George Clooney, for highly desirable lakeside properties.

For over a year we had little hope that we would be able to claw our way out of our melancholy. Then, from out of the blue, a minor miracle happened, when an attractive three-bedroom property appeared on an estate agent's web site. It was a three-floored villa, built into the mountainside, just forty metres from the lake road. It had a separate one-bedroom apartment on the first floor, terraced gardens, wide balconies, a garage and a spectacular, twenty-seven kilometre wide view from north to south over the magnificent Lake. This was a property we could really get excited about, especially as it was one we could actually afford. All this and it was only ten kilometres further up the Lake from Moltrasio, in the appealing, lively and unspoilt village of Argegno. After five months of bureaucracy we became the proud owners of the villa.

We had already realised that saying goodbye to Moltrasio and its residents was not going to be easy. In the thirteen years we had lived there we had become extremely fond of the place and our neighbours regarded us as part of their family. We were looking forward to living in our own home in Argegno with our four adopted cats, but on our last day there were tears aplenty as we said our farewells to our friends. They said they would miss us; it was as if we were letting them down by leaving the village. We tried to assure them that we would be back to see them and I tried to make light of the situation by repeating we were only moving down the road, and that it was purely for economic reasons. Nicola did persuade some of the younger ones that we had been forced out by circumstances, but we knew the older generation were not convinced. The historical mountainous nature of Italy splits the country into hundreds of neighbourhoods. Being virtually isolated, each village around Lake Como has its own identity therefore, small communities are very close-knit. Even with the advent of modern day communications and the effects of access to the outside world that this brings, if anybody becomes accepted in such a community, it is not easy for them to turn away.

2 Arrivati

The first thing we had to do on our arrival in Argegno was to select what we wanted of the furniture we had inherited along with the villa. Our apartment in Moltrasio had only one bedroom, so our limited amount of furniture wasn't anywhere near enough to furnish a large villa. The villa had an extensive run of wardrobes in one of the bedrooms, a double bed and an L-shaped divan in the lounge, which all came in handy until we had time to replace them. Because the previous owners had moved to an apartment without a garden they had also left a complete set of outside furniture and a pile of gardening equipment we found very welcome.

Our second task, which was more essential than getting the villa sorted out was to meet the neighbours, because we had already heard that the locals were interested to learn about the two *Moltrasini* who had moved in. Word had preceded us because our friends, Sandra and her husband Gherado were eager to introduce us into their community. We knew them from reunions at a hotel they once owned near to Moltrasio prior to their retirement, and until recently we hadn't seen them for nearly twelve years. Sandra was Scottish and Gherado was born and bred in Argegno, so Nicola had been in touch with them to tell them that we would soon be neighbours.

Gherado in particular was most helpful in enlightening inquisitive residents about us, and while Nicola was working in Milan he introduced me into the Bar Onda society, where he and the majority of local men hung out to pass the time of day. It was a case of déjà vu, because it was almost the same scene as the one I had become accustomed to in the Bar Centrale in Moltrasio.

The one thing that gave me some security when I did meet the local men in the bar was that I could now speak Italian and I could actually communicate with them. Thirteen years previously, when we first moved to Moltrasio and the locals spoke to me, I used to just smile and nod agreeably at I knew not what. However, under some circumstances learning to speak Italian in Italy is not always an advantage. The locals in the Bar Onda prefer to converse in their own dialect, which is very different from Italian and different again from the dialect in Moltrasio. Trying to learn a dialect is extremely difficult if a person is not brought up listening to it. Apart from the occasional abbreviated Italian word, dialects seem to comprise of a lot of grunts. After the exhaustive struggle I'd had in order to learn Italian to an acceptable standard I found the locals, known as Argegnini, were telling me to forget about Italian and learn to speak their dialect.

I particularly enjoyed the weekly *il club di lunedi* (the Monday club), a strictly men-only affair, held in the Bar Onda. It was also referred to as the 'church-going club', because those in attendance told their wives they were going to the late morning mass in the village church, rather than the real reason, which was to escape from home for a few hours. The members were Gherado and half a dozen of his retired mates, plus another half a dozen working restaurateurs from the area, whose day off was Monday. And they would all meet up at eleven o'clock in the morning to discuss every subject imaginable, but mainly it was to have *aperitivi* (aperitifs), before lunch; when they would consume several bottles of vino, accompanied by several plates of *salume* (sliced cold meats) with black olives, wild onions, duck pâté on panini or warm focaccia and *alici marinate in olio di oliva* (fresh anchovies in olive oil).

~~~

A couple of weeks after we'd moved into our new home, we had a visit from our nearest neighbour, who lived half a kilometre away. He introduced himself as Vittorio, a sprightly chain-smoker who told us he was born in Argegno, seventy years ago. He also informed us that thirty-four years earlier he had sold an acre of his land to the man who built our villa. Vittorio happened to be one of a largish group of energetic, retired men who occupied the seats around the village fountain in piazza Roma, the central piazza in the village and he invited me to join him and his friends for their daily pre-lunch aperitivi around the fountain. This was a slightly different group from the Monday Club, because although some of them do attend both unions, all the members of the group that meet around the fountain are retired. Unfortunately for Nicola, Vittorio didn't include her in his invitation. He was sorry to inform her that it was, like the Monday Club, strictly for men only.

The village fountain is a sturdy granite structure, surrounded by a circular granite seat that has been polished to a high gloss from the amount of use it gets. The fountain is set plumb in the middle of the piazza and is enclosed on three sides by tall, narrow, buildings that are centuries old. Besides shops, the buildings house several bars with rented apartments above and some excellent trattorie, one of them offering hotel accommodation. The open side has the same spectacular view of the lake as the one we have from our villa. Like most Italian village piazzas, piazza Roma is the principal area for villagers to meet and exchange local news and gossip. The one in Argegno is also the place where the weekly market is held, selling household articles, clothes, leather goods and a lot of food and wine.

The buildings around the piazza have been decorated sympathetically in muted colours that have mellowed with age; pale, sun-bleached golden ochre alternates with sky blue, rose pink, raw sienna and terra cotta, which gives the place a harmonious appearance. All the window shutters and the doors are painted in one of a range of regulation colours; Brunswick green, sepia or dark chocolate. Anybody who wishes to repaint their premises in a different colour has to apply to the *Municipio* (the town hall) for permission and it won't be granted unless they choose the new colour from this selection. This wise regulation was put in place because of the many blunders the injudicious can make when left to their own devices.

Every day, and well into the evenings residents and tourists alike enjoy desserts, snacks and coffee in the piazza, or in the case of Vittorio and his mates a few glasses of something a little stronger. The romantic could view any one of hundreds of Italian villages like Argegno through rose-tinted spectacles, because they are unquestionably picturesque, but what goes on beneath the façade that is piazza Roma is not, on certain days at least, all sweetness and light.

Visitors to Argegno who arrive before lunch may notice a group of old men seated around the fountain. It is also more than likely that the visitors won't take much heed of them, but if the visitors do notice them, they will see them playing cards and drinking wine and when they look at their sun-tanned faces they will probably think, like I did when I first met them that they are a kindly bunch. If our visitors do think that, they will have been much mistaken.

Each and every day, these old boys meet. They are

fixtures on the landscape and are the eyes and ears of the village and sometimes the instigators of the local hearsay. With an average age of seventy-two, apart from Lorenzo, they were all at one time involved in the catering trade. In their days the were either hotel proprietors, bar owners, restaurateurs, chefs, barmen, cooks, waiters, food wholesalers and the like. At first glance they are difficult to tell apart. Some are shorter than average, although a couple of them, like Vittorio are taller. Some are slimmer, but although Mario is the tubbiest, none of them could be described as fat. Two have full heads of hair, most have receding hairlines, but Mario alone is bald. Style and appearance is, and always has been of great importance to the Italian male, and that doesn't diminish with age. All of our group dress uniformly, in starched shirts, either white or with maybe a fine vertical stripe of the palest blue or pink, with a monogrammed top pocket, worn unbuttoned to the second button down. Trousers - never shorts - will be of a lightweight material. The colour is a matter of taste, but like the buildings that surround them, they will be from a limited range of shades; generally grey, cream, navy blue or fawn is preferred and always worn with a belt. Shoes will be slip-on, perhaps brown one day and black another.

I've got to know most of them fairly well, but I'm still not part of their inner circle, and never will be. They have far too much shared history for that to happen. They have more to tell each other than they tell me, and even that appears to be shrouded in confidentiality. Although I don't say so directly to their faces, I sometimes refer to them as *monelli* (mischievous types), because if they are not watched, that's what they can be. They may be old, but they still act like boys and after spending only a short time in their company I discovered that, on sunny days in particular they rarely let a good looking woman pass by without making comment. This, I have to say surprised me because I had thought old men were past that sort of thing. The seating arrangement that encircles the fountain, is set directly opposite the jetty where the public ferries boats that ply across the lake stop, and is ideally positioned for the old boys to allow their imaginations to let rip. Each time a ferry docks, the old boys break off from their card game to see what attractive ladies may have arrived.

Imagine now, if you will, a morning with them, to gain an insight into what draws them to the same spot, day after day. The lake is an enticing cerulean blue and a brilliant, phosphorescent sparkle comes off it as the sun hits its centre. It is too bright to look at for long. In sharp contrast, the shadows of the buildings in the main piazza are almost pitch-black, as are the contours of the plane trees that shade the pavement. Underneath their branches sit fishermen, bent over as they cast their bait, looking for all the world as if they are related to the trees. To the left of the lake the perch jump and the fishermen swing their rods in synchronisation towards the diminishing ripples. On this occasion they are too late, because the fish saw them before they did. Across the road from the fishermen, the old boys are still rooted to the seat around the fountain. They will tell anybody who should ask them that anglers are a breed unto themselves, with no other interests in life beyond freshwater fish. I don't want to spoil their hypothesising, but if somebody should ask them what other interests they have in life, apart from flights of fancy about unattainable females, they'd be hard pushed to come up with anything.

Five minutes ago a ferry docked: one particular lady walked off it and wandered into the piazza, occasionally stopping to look in the windows of the clothes shops and at the menus outside the trattorie. Ten pairs of eyes follow her, but she is not intimidated by this, nor the murmuring and pointing that accompanies their gaze. Our visitor is blonde, so their opinion is that she is German, or she could be Scandinavian. None of them are sure, and their opinions change by the second. A natural blonde is a novelty in Italy, so this one is conspicuous. The thought of having a relationship with a genuine blonde seems to do for the Italian male what the contemplation of a liaison with a French girl does for the British male. It seems exotic: if an Italian woman is blonde then it is more than likely her colouring will have come out of a bottle.

Somebody suggests that Alessandro, the cheekiest of the bunch asks her where she's from, because he knows a smattering of a number of languages. Besides, nobody else has got the courage to go and make conversation with the visitor, in case there's a language barrier. But we find he's missing. His wife had phoned him earlier with instructions to buy some vegetables from the food market, so the opportunity to find out about the visitor is fading. In fact it has vanished, because she's gone into the tourist information centre. Ten minutes later she reappears, but it seems I am the only one who has noticed because the card game has reached fever pitch and money is about to be lost, so concentrations are focused on the table. The ferry is returning and the blonde is making her way back to the landing stage. There she goes, melting away like warm gelato.

After a period of inaction, the wily and wiry Alessandro, having done his wife's errands re-joins the band to howls of derision about being under her thumb. But he gets his own back when he tells them that he spoke to the blonde lady who got off the boat. He had asked her if there was anything she wanted while she was in the village. It transpires that she was Swedish and married and her husband would be arriving the next day to join her on holiday in Bellagio. Alessandro doesn't flinch when it comes to women. They are his hobby and if there's a whiff of perfume in the air he's off in a flash to see who is wearing it. He's only interested in women and football (in that order) and for him, it is all about scoring. He is sixty-nine, with a receding hairline and whitened teeth that glow, yet despite these obvious marks of age, the habit of a lifetime of pursuit still persists. Or, maybe it's all to impress his mates and he pretends to be the potent force he says he once was. I must say, on close inspection of him at work, female visitors who arrive within a stones throw distance of the piazza fountain are blissfully unaware that he is not particular about the age of the women he targets. As long as they are wearing a skirt, they are fair game to him. A single woman of sixty he will honour. Towards a woman of forty or fifty his sun-tanned face will bear a smile of familiarity and he will become incorrigibly excited. For a woman in her thirties or younger he will act as if he's known her all his life and with a ring-of-confidence smile he will let her know he is the icon of maturity she has been searching for all her life.

For all his and his friends daydreaming about affairs they would love to have with the foreign women who visit Argegno, old age has snuck up on the old boys faster than they have realised. It has brought with it a load of common problems, and they deal them out in a discussion about them like a bad hand of cards, whilst coughing, spluttering, smiling, laughing and cursing them out loud. 'Why,' they want to know 'are we are trapped in a beautiful cage besides the most majestic lake in Italy, when all the good it is for us is to aid a successful drowning? We have inhaled the air that floats above it since our first day. The lake is where we have always been, but the world has moved on, whilst we have remained steadfast. Why are we stuck with this baggage? Why have we been devoted to Argegno, when the world is so large and there are thousands of fountains for us to reflect beside? If we had our time again, would we chew the fat with the same comrades? And will the next generation be as steadfast after we've gone?' They all ponder these same questions several times a day, but the one they cannot resolve is finding a restorative for their lost virility. More than anything, they want a final fling with a beautifully bronzed blonde dream before their brain cells dissolve and their bodies disintegrate.

Chubby, bald, Mario has arrived to join them. He was a restaurateur, but sold his business for more than it was worth and promptly retired. According to the grapevine, he now has so much money he doesn't know what to do with it. His life has always been spent within the vicinity of the fountain and now he has the opportunity to spend the money he's worked all his life for, he doesn't know how to do it. Alongside his state and private pensions he makes a sizeable income renting out the four luxury apartments he owns to tourists and a shop he owns to a florist. He did own a bar until a bank made him a substantial offer to convert it into one of their branches. The same bank also advised him on some excellent long-term investments; so he now makes even more money on top of the stash he doesn't know what to do with. For fun we all kid him that he is so wealthy he owns his own bank.

I can feel him looming behind me. He thinks I'm sketching, and I know he wants to look over my shoulder. In fact I'm making notes about what he and his friends are saying so I can put them in this book. To satisfy his curiosity I let him have a peep at what I'm doing but now he's seen words instead of images he's lost interest. For the sake of courtesy he asks me what I'm writing, but I cannot tell him or he'll want me to spell it out to them, so I tell him it's a letter to a friend.

Four ladies in their fifties, whom we think are American are approaching the fountain with a map and an enquiring look in their eyes, but the old boys are noticeably reluctant to help. Vittorio must have felt sorry for them, because he's pointed them in the direction of the tourist information office. If the women had been twenty years younger the entire group would have smothered them with attention and they'd have been invited to sit down to share a bottle of Bonarda.

After the Americans have left, two more women arrive in the piazza. They look at us intently for a few seconds and we begin to speculate about which one of us they are interested in. Luigi whispers to Guido, loudly enough for us to hear, but softly enough so the women can't, that Guido's flies are undone. Alessandro steps forward to find out what language they speak. He asks them in German, but they reply in French that they are Flemish. They are not at all interested in any of us, but rather they are trying to look at the village fountain. One of them then says they have read about its history and have travelled to Argegno especially to see it, and now we are blocking their view. So, as gentlemen are supposed to do, we all rise up and move to one side to let them feast their eyes on an object that we feel doesn't warrant the scrutiny they are giving it, and we chat amongst ourselves until the women have seen enough. To find out what it is that is so special about the fountain, two of our company stand alongside the two women, following their line of vision. By the expression on their faces they return none the wiser about what is so special about this lump of grey granite, which dribbles, rather than shoots water into the air, as a proper fountain should (that is, until there is a *festa nazionale*, a public holiday when the Municipio turns the pressure up and soaks every visitor to the main piazza within a five-metre radius). Mario says that in all his seventy-two years he has never really looked at it properly until now.

The women take some photographs of the fountain and Alessandro gets himself further involved with them by giving them the benefit of his knowledge about it. In French, he says, 'the original fountain was much taller than the present one and it was made of cast iron, but it fell to bits through neglect in the 1930s. Its replacement was built by a famous architect who was trying to copy the style of the period, but in granite.' He is about to offer the women some more information, but one of them interrupts him, asking him the name of the famous architect. Alessandro says he doesn't know, and she chastises him for his inadequacy. As a form of protection, Alessandro changes his story and says that he does actually know the architect's name but he has momentarily forgotten it. The woman wrinkles her nose horribly at him, saying that she knows the architect's name - Botteri - because she has been researching the fountain. 'If you should ever volunteer information about this fountain to foreign visitors,' she tells him, 'then you should make sure you can relay the facts properly.'

Lorenzo is one of the old boys whom I had thought was less of a *monello* than the others. He's a retired *Guardia di Finanza*, (finance policeman) and now he is a part-time taxi driver. Although he's outnumbered nine to one by retired hospitality trade members he's accepted amongst them, because in a way he was one of them. When, as a member of the fraud squad he wore a smart khaki uniform. He was responsible for checking out the accounts of the various restaurateurs, hoteliers, barkeepers and the like around the village. If he found any misdemeanours, he had the power to levy considerable fines. To get around any indiscretions he may have unearthed as he turned over the pages of their spurious balance sheets, the proprietors found that if they entertained him and his good lady wife lavishly, providing of course all the accompanying beverages, he could be persuaded to look the other way.

I've noticed on several occasions that if there is an eye-catching female tourist wandering around town Lorenzo will, unlike the rest of them hardly register an interest in her. He always seems to be keener on clearing up his winnings from the last hand of cards and getting another one underway than waste time staring at the unobtainable. But Pino, formerly the manager of the bar at Como railway station put me straight about Lorenzo. In Pino's estimation Lorenzo is the most immoral of them all. Apparently he owns a second home on the island of Capri that he lets out free of charge to two middle-aged women. He visits the island in the spring and in the summer to collect what they owe him, and it's not money. Before he sets off from Argegno, he informs his wife he's going on a deep-sea fishing trip with some friends and he keeps his fishing tackle in his garage as his cover. When the time comes for him to leave, he tells his wife how much he loves her and how much he's looking forward to the lure of salt water and hauling in kilos of tuna. He'll then ask her to help him pack his waterproof gear and tie his tackle onto the roof of his car until she's bored, but the truth is, that's where it will remain all the time he is away. According to Pino, Lorenzo has never been on a fishing trip in his life. He doesn't know one end of a fishing rod from the other, but he certainly knows one end of a woman from the other.

The next person to turn up, or rather, return, as he had been here earlier is Giuseppe, His nickname is *Il Americano* - The American. He is the second tallest of the group, but he is a little run down these days, which seems to be the result of something progressive. I don't think it's unfair to say he is the least well dressed of the group. The older old boys call him Pepe to his face, but the younger old boys regularly call him *Americano*. He got his nickname from the decades he worked as a waiter in New York City's Little Italy. When he retired, he came back to Argegno, his birthplace. On this particular morning, Pepe seems much friendlier than usual and he kisses most of the assembled on the sides of their faces. Then as the morning aperitivi session progresses he suddenly singles me out, coaxing me away from the main group to a shaded corner of the piazza outside the gelateria, where he says he wants to talk to me in confidence.

'Living here,' he says, 'is like living in Limbo-land!'

I ask him if he knows of a place that nobody else does, but the quip seems to confuse him and he ignores it. Half an hour earlier, when he first arrived for the union he didn't seem to be under the influence of alcohol, but he does now. He comes close to me, as if perhaps he thinks I am hard of hearing - so close in fact that the stench of warm vino on his breath takes mine away. I later discover that he's been at the bottle since the Bar Onda opened at 6.30 this morning. It's now 11.30. When he seems certain that I will stay put to listen, he takes two photographs out of his wallet and shows them to me. One is of his ex-wife, the other of his son and daughter. 'All gone,' he says. 'And it's my own fault. I don't know where they are.'

The photographs are dog-eared, sad-looking things, badly faded with chewed corners and deep creases. The one of his ex-wife has a tear across her neck, as if her throat has been slashed. He says his son is abroad, but he doesn't know in which country and his daughter is in London but he doesn't know in which area. 'Perhaps you recognise her?' he asks. 'The photograph was taken forty years ago, when she was eight. I know it's a long shot, but you might have seen her.'

I agree that it was a long shot, and tell him I don't recognise her.

'You see,' he continues, 'today is her birthday.'

Trying to make light of his sadness, I say it must make her nine. Fortunately, he isn't too obsessed about his absent family, which is a relief in itself, but what he really wants to talk about is his concern about the plight in which Italy finds herself, stuck in an insecure Europe and threatened by the Chinese takeover of her trade and industry. Why he's chosen me specifically to talk about a subject I am unfamiliar with and even less interested in is odd, but as his monologue progresses I realise the retired waiter is an active, self-taught academic who is trying his hardest not to be remembered as a has-been, or to give up the fight. Now, in his twilight years he has the time to think constructively and his aim is to rectify the mistakes of others. He doesn't want to be remembered solely for clearing away dirty dinner plates. He wants to learn from the errors of others and impart his insight for the rest of mankind to reflect upon. As a thinker, combined with the strength of a rebel, he hopes he has the power to move mountains. He says he needs help to fulfil his mission, and this is where I come in. In other words, because I am younger, he wants to place his burden upon my shoulders and have me carry on the task after he has gone. Once again he fumbles inside his tatty leather wallet and pulls out a scrap of notepaper with some words scribbled on it. These, it seems are to demonstrate to the world that Italy is not the spent force a lot of people think it is and he wants me to make sure his generation is not entirely to blame for its erosion.

'We are hanging on,' he muses, 'and the tears of an old man are being shed to halt the puerility of our age. Brussels is the ruin of us. They are pulling us apart and giving us away. It is your responsibility along with everyone else's to prise us away before we are spent. You and your generation are involved in a war and you are not responding to the threat. At the moment we have been hoodwinked. We are content with false greed. A few make hay and the rest try to follow, but the Chinese are not playing games. In ten years from now they will be riding roughshod over us. They have a goal and we don't, and when they are ready they will wipe us away with the stroke of a pen. They will buy out the jerks in Brussels then pay off the worthless industrialists in a worthless currency. To bring them to heel we must impose trade sanctions, but how can we implement them when they own us? Our expertise and our manufacturing base will be in their hands and they will be the ones supplying us with what we need.'

But in the sky, a storm is brewing, and within ten minutes a vast black shroud of altocumulus clouds has gathered. The humidity level is high and we need the heavy rain the clouds promise to rinse away stale sweat. We need the mornings to be fresh, and I need to be rid of Pepe and his blather *presto*. I say to him I'll rally the troops immediately and we'll hit the Euro MEPs first thing tomorrow to demand they develop an antidote to the Chinese.

But he isn't done yet. He says he can't send this rough note to the local newspaper. He wants me to convert it into comprehensible language and then e-mail it to them, because he cannot type or use a computer and he wants a copy of it by the following day. Fortunately, heavy, spaced-out raindrops start to cluster around us, so I escort him to the Bar Onda and then retreat to the greengrocer's across the medieval stone footbridge that spans the river Telo. I hide amongst a group of sheltering tourists in case there is something else Pepe wants me to do.

3 A Challenging Art Commission

One mid-week afternoon during our first winter in Argegno as I was pruning the trees and bushes in the garden, I received a phone call. The caller said his name was Nardo. I didn't know who he was, but he had a voice like a congested toad and told me he was calling from Campione d'Italia, which is a tiny Italian enclave in the Swiss canton of Ticino, on the banks of Lake Lugano, near the Italian border. He said he was looking for an artist to do some work, and I had been recommended to him by the owner of the shop I buy my paint materials from in Como. He said he wanted to meet me that same evening, and so he could offer me dinner in his restaurant I had to be there on the stroke of twenty-one hundred hours. I was reluctant to take up an offer of dinner from someone I didn't know before I'd had the opportunity to find out more about him, especially someone who sounded foreboding. I told him that I had already prepared dinner and I was waiting for my wife's arrival from work, but to keep the man interested and not appear ungrateful for his offer of work, I tried to get him to change the appointment to the following morning. But he insisted I had to meet him at nine sharp that evening, or else he would look for somebody else. When I said Nicola would be expecting dinner when she arrived home, he told me to bring her as well.

Campione d'Italia is very different from the rest of Italy. Situated twenty-eight kilometres north of Como, it is Italian sovereign territory, but anybody wishing to enter from Italy has to go through Swiss passport control, and then go through Italian passport control. But though Campione is Italian, the currency is the Swiss Franc and the cars carry Swiss registration plates. The residents are tax-exempt on the first two hundred thousand francs they earn and they are not required to pay community taxes. They are also exempt from IVA, the Italian equivalent of Value Added Tax because the town's vast gambling casino generates enough revenue to keep the Italian tax authorities happy and to allow the population to live in expensive properties virtually tax-free. All the banks are Swiss owned, and Swiss banking rules prevail.

Down through history, Italy has been one of the biggest, if not the biggest influence on the world of gambling. The betting laws and customs in most of Western Europe and the Americas are derived from those of Italy. According to centuries-old accounts, Italy adopted the fortune-telling tarocco cards - the forerunner of our modern tarot cards off the invading Saracens, then used them for gambling. Baccarat was invented in Italy, most likely toward the end of the fifteenth century and lotto, the game that would later evolve into bingo, appeared around the same time. Casinos appeared in Venice in the early seventeenth century - the word itself is Italian - and in 1933, Mussolini permitted the building of the casino in Campione. Because casinos were banned in Switzerland in 1921, and because the casino was so close to the Swiss border, Campione profited handsomely from the Swiss ban. The ban on casinos in Switzerland was lifted in 2000 and it now has nineteen, which is many more than Italy has. There is also a ban on sports betting in Switzerland, although many citizens engage in it through on-line betting. (Incidentally, in the Swiss town of Ruswil there is an annual game called Cow Bingo, in which betting is allowed. Seven hundred and fifty squares are marked out in a field and numbered, turning the field into a giant bingo card. The gamblers place bets on a square of their choice, then a herd of cows is turned into the field. The winning square is the one upon which the most number of cow pats have been deposited.)

With the biggest casino in Europe - it has three hundred and fifty slot machines and thirty-two poker and gaming tables - some many-starred hotels, expensive restaurants and plenty of flashing lights, Campione is like a mini Las Vegas. It is unashamedly renowned as a haven for offshore investments and tax avoidance schemes. It is also ideally positioned as a handy spot for transferring large amounts of unofficial revenue from Italy into numbered Swiss bank accounts. Around the time Italy joined the European Union Monetary System, the banks became jittery over accusations of them being involved in the transfer of illicit cash, especially when handling cross border currency transactions. Although Campione's illegal money-laundering set-ups are gone, if somebody says they have business connections there, eyebrows will be raised. So, when this potential client telephoned, saying he owned a restaurant in Campione, my suspicions were immediately aroused.

Two hours after the phone call, Nicola arrived home from Milan after a hard day at work. When I told her about the edgy conversation I'd had with this Nardo character, I thought that she would turn her nose up at the suggestion of eating out, but she was surprisingly up-beat about it; in fact, she seemed quite excited. She knew that the opportunity to view a millionaire's recreation ground like Campione d'Italia, and to eat there doesn't come often unless you can afford it. So, off we set.

Campione comes alive at night. At the edge of the town is an impressive archway, with the words "This is Campione" spelt out in lights. Within a few hundred metres of driving through the arch we passed the casino, its mock Grecian façade decked out in flashing coloured lights. It stood out like a throbbing, sore thumb. In the half-light it appeared to have been painted a gaudy pink, a contrast to the sun-bleached stone of the Parthenon in Athens, on which it had probably been modelled. It was an example of expensive tackiness, which I suppose is better than cheap tackiness. Nicola insisted that I stopped the car across the road from the casino entrance for a few moments, so we could both gawp at the gamblers arriving. We watched them emerge from behind the tinted windows of their foreign-registered Porsches, stretch Mercedes and BMWs to wager over the roulette, chemin de fer, baccarat, blackjack and poker tables. We set off again and I struggled to steer our second-hand Fiat Brava up and down the steep, narrow one-way streets and awkward T-junctions, looking for a place to park. After doing two circuits of the town, we eventually found the only available space in a darkened street, well away from the bright lights. But where was the restaurant? Nardo had told me to look for a red door with a brass bell-pull to the right side of it, but even after a further phone call to him, we still couldn't find it. We found a police officer, who gave us clearer directions. I had been looking for a restaurant window with maybe the proprietors name written above it and people sitting inside it eating, but it turned out it wasn't that type of restaurant.

In the half-light we found the red door, set in a plain rendered wall. There was a card swipe slot fixed to its frame, to enable members, and no one else to enter. As we weren't members, I pulled a brass knob on the door, which rang a bell inside. There was a longish pause, then, suddenly a spy-hole, set at face height slid open, just like in a speakeasy in an old Hollywood gangster film. An eye appeared in the spy hole and peered at us. Then the hole was slammed shut and there was the sound of a key turning in a lock. After another longish pause, the door swung open to reveal a large man with an equally large head. He was dressed in a black suit, white shirt and black bow tie. Without a word, he beckoned us to follow him up a long flight of dimly lit stairs, which led into an equally dimly lit but spacious room with a low slung ceiling, filled with dining tables. The man pointed us towards the back of the room, where there was a large, circular dining table with a pull-down light suspended over it.

The place smelt like a restaurant, and a good one at that, even though it appeared to be devoid of clientele or waiters. The light didn't get much brighter until we arrived at the large table, where a little man in a charcoal grey suit with a bow tie and an equally grey complexion sat eating. This, it appeared was Nardo. He gesticulated with his fork for us to come closer. When we met, he shook my hand, but not convincingly, and he didn't bother to stand up. When I introduced Nicola, he hardly acknowledged her. Also seated at the table were three other mysterious looking men. They were much bigger than Nardo, and they too wore dark suits and bow ties and they also looked grey. We were joined by the man with the large head who had let us in, but it took Nardo a second or so before he got around to introducing him and the rest of this intimidating group. This he did with a flick of his wrist as he mumbled their names. A gesture that gave me the impression that they weren't really friends of his at all.

We had arrived on the stroke of nine o'clock, as the man had ordered, but they had already started to eat. Nardo told us that we had missed two of the starters because we were late. I didn't want to argue, and out of courtesy I apologised, but neither he nor anyone else acknowledged what I said. Nardo simply gave another flick of his wrist to indicate that Nicola and I should be seated. We sat, and the sight of the food told me it was of the highest quality. The menu, which he'd chosen for us without any discussion beforehand, contained twelve courses. Two obliging and gracious waiters were kept busy wheeling the trolleys around as we tucked wholeheartedly into quince, partridge, poussin, quail, Aberdeen Angus steak, Scottish smoked salmon with caviar, wine, champagne, desserts and coffee.

As the courses arrived, Nicola and I enthused to the company present about how wonderful they all smelt and tasted. In spite of this, it became evident that the atmosphere around the meal table was a total contrast to the warm, delightful food and totally unlike what we had become accustomed to when eating out in Italy. In fact, I'd go as far as to say there was no atmosphere at all. It was as if I had imagined the urgent tone in Nardo's voice when he telephoned me. I had anticipated that I would be sitting next to him, discussing what it was he wanted me to paint. Such a discussion wasn't possible because of the seating arrangement, so I contented myself with the idea that we would talk when the food was over.

I noticed that some of his friends didn't speak at all during the entire two hours that we were in their presence. Instead, they kept their faces pressed low over their plates, and those that did speak kept their conversation to the minimum necessary between themselves. They didn't pass a single comment about the outstanding food. They could have been eating beans on toast for all the admiration they gave it. Possibly they ate like this every night of the week. I concluded from all this that Nardo was making sure I knew he was unquestionably the boss. He had an aura of fearsome magnetism and nobody was allowed to speak unless they had been spoken to first. Who the others at the table were, and how they were connected to each other as a group I wasn't told, and I didn't ask. But I got the impression early on that they were all "yes" men. One of them kept answering Nardo's cell phone, then handing it to Nardo. When Nardo had finished speaking, he would hand it back, with the instruction to 'phone certain names, but not in our company. So, this man kept leaving the room halfway through eating, returning to find that his food had gone cold or that he had missed out on the next course.

Nevertheless, Nicola and I still tried to liven up an almost eerie atmosphere around the table by continuing to show our appreciation for such magnificent food and luxurious living, but Nardo would just look at us as if we were infantile. This angered me, because he came across as being ill-mannered, but I kept my cool because I was interested to see where all this was going to lead. It didn't matter to me if I got a commission out of the evening's meeting or not, because my programme had been to work on our extensive garden, so I intended enjoying the evening, and if necessary I would say what I felt when the time came. If this Nardo character expected me to kowtow to him and remain silent like the members of his brigade seemed to be doing, he was mistaken.

Nardo's attitude reminded me of a Como architect with whom I'd had too many run-ins over art projects and payment difficulties in the past, and I couldn't help wondering if this was going to be a repeat performance. Like the Como architect, Nardo had no sense of humour, or if he had then he kept it well hidden. But I was prepared to go along with what I might have got myself into because I could have been wrong. If nothing else, I was eating some of the most extravagant food I'd ever tasted, so I thought I'd give the guy a chance before condemning him.

Two hours later, the meal was over and I thought Nardo would now want to talk business. But to my surprise he asked me if I knew my way to Bedano, because that was where the job was. I said I'd never heard of the place, so he told me to follow his car. Nardo and his four friends left in a fleet of extravagant saloon cars, with us two in our little Fiat at the tail end, trying to keep up.

Bedano is in Switzerland, a thirty-minute drive from Campione. After driving through its meandering one-way streets, we arrived outside another mysterious door. This one was varnished oak, rather than red, but it had the obligatory sliding hatch. And like the red door, it had a huge number of locking mechanisms that had to be operated before the door could be opened and we could all get in. But rather than leading to a restaurant, this side door led to a "night". This is the name that Italians give to any type of place that opens its doors after midnight. It can be a straightforward nightclub, an after-hours drinking club, a lap-dancing club or a strip joint. This place was a brothel. Nardo was the owner and his assistant, the one who had been doing the telephoning during the meal, was the manager. The man with the large head was the doorman, the fourth was the barman and the last of the quintet was the bouncer.

We arrived in Bedano on the stroke of midnight, just as the club opened and Nardo and his friends were beginning their working day. What to Nicola and me had been a late dinner had been their breakfast. Immediately we arrived, Nardo told us to sit at the bar on high stools, where we were served cocktails. He clicked his fingers to signal his bouncer to invite in half a dozen punters from the lobby to sit at the bar. Another click of Nardo's fingers brought six partly-clad women from a back room, and another click had them drooling over the punters. Nicola was astonished to realise where she'd ended up. It was patently obvious to her and to everybody in the place that she was the only fully clothed female in the place. I assured her I had absolutely no prior knowledge of why or what we were doing in a house of ill repute, but she kept looking at me mighty suspiciously. I couldn't discuss this in depth with her at the time, because we were in close contact with those around us, but it was noticeable that every time one of the "working girls" or Nardo came near her, she clasped her hands around the fur collar of her coat and pulled it together across her chest to protect her modesty. The temperature inside the 'night' rose noticeably and lingered around the twenty-five degree mark, but when Nardo asked Nicola if she wanted to remove her coat so she would be more comfortable, she refused nervously and hung onto it for all she was worth. On the expectation she would be attending a smart dinner in his restaurant, she had chosen to wear a fairly skimpy cocktail dress, so she didn't want to reveal any sign of flesh in case she was mistaken for something she wasn't.

Surely, I thought, I must be the first man ever to have escorted his wife to a brothel.

With the arrival of more clients, at least another eight partly clad women appeared from the back room and began parading in front of them. Soon after them I counted another five gentlemen callers arriving in the space of fifteen minutes who began to engage actively with the "working girls." I sensed Nicola shiver and she gripped my hand as one of the unengaged girls, who was sitting next to her at the bar, persuaded yet another night caller to open his wallet by stroking her exposed nipple across the side of his cheek. He bit into it like a hungry wolf. There were still five girls loitering with intent around the bar, all-smiling, but Nardo wasn't smiling. He didn't seem to be capable of doing so; his face was set with a mask of sallow seriousness, a permanent, fixed grimace. He seemed to be a worrier by nature and by the sign of things a redoubtable operator. Suddenly, something displeased him and with an agitated flick of his wrist he left my company for a few seconds to "kick ass". I think one of his girls was slow to respond to the advances of a patron with a humped back. He had chosen this girl, but she hadn't stepped forward and he'd complained to her boss.

Nardo flicked his wrist once again and pointed one of his girls in my direction, but it was only to ask me what else we wanted to drink. It was service with a beaming smile, Bedano style. What now? I thought. In his husky voice, Nardo at last began talking to me about how he wanted me to transform the look of the interior of his club. He said he wanted something different from what he already had, and asked me if I had any ideas. Before I came up with any I pointed out to him the practical difficulties of working in Switzerland on a daily basis. I was concerned about crossing the border in my car with a stack of paint materials inside it and ladders tied to the roof-rack, and if that wouldn't be conspicuous enough, what about the correct documentation and tax paraphernalia I'd need to stay on the right side the law?

'No problem,' he said. 'One of my friends is a Customs officer and he can issue you with the correct papers so you can pass through the border unhindered.'

He then suggested an alternative. 'If you are feeling uncomfortable about working in Switzerland,' he said, 'perhaps you should consider renting an apartment close by while the work is being undertaken.'

Up until this point we hadn't yet discussed money. I wondered how much he would be prepared to pay me in subsistence so I could afford to rent an apartment, but as I was about to ask him, he interrupted me so he could match more of his girls with more gentlemen callers. He than said his intention was to close the club doors in a week's time, then, after a minimum refit that would include new furniture and my painted artwork, he wanted to reopen the premises one month later as a disco and lap-dancing club.

So that was the theme. I'd been stuck until then as to know what to paint, because decorating brothel interiors wasn't my forte, but after understanding that he wanted murals around the proposed disco area, I suggested a series of large action portraits of past and present pop stars. Nardo produced a twenty-metre long tape measure and instructed me to take hold of the end of it while he directed operations around a pole-dancer performing on the stage area and a client and one of his girls engaged in the club's raison d'etre on an Empire style chaise-longue. As I was about to follow Nardo, Nicola grabbed my arm and pleaded with me not to leave her alone at the bar, so I got her to hold the end of Nardo's tape while I wrote down the measurements in my notebook.

We left this bizarre scenario just after two o'clock in the morning, with the agreement that I would email him in three days' time with the designs and a price for four large panels for the proposed disco area that I would paint in my studio and then have delivered by courier service to Switzerland. This way I would not have to commute across the border every day to work illegally, and he wouldn't have to pay the cost of my travel or a three-week stay in an apartment.

From past experience, I know that Italians like to have a nice *sconto* - a discount - when it comes to buying something and Nardo informed me, before I'd even started preparing the designs that he would expect one if he paid me in cash. A sconto can range from ten to fifty per cent, depending on how persuasive the buyer is or how desperate the vendor is. Three days later, after I'd emailed my sketches to Nardo I found out, as I had anticipated, that I had a battle on my hands over money and that included just how much sconto he wanted. Nardo was the pushy type, without scruple. It was written all over him and the second I met him I knew I was probably going to have difficulty doing business with him. When he telephoned me, after he'd downloaded the designs I'd emailed, I stuck out for a twenty five per cent sconto. He told me so in no uncertain terms that he wasn't happy with that. He then told me to reconsider the deal, with me offering him a fifty per cent discount and if I did, he would throw in a twelve-course dinner for two in his restaurant in Campione, or I could have a full-blown sex session with a girl of my choice in his brothel. It was now my turn to be unhappy and I told him so in equally certain terms. In the end there was no agreement and we left it where I would phone him again when I'd thought about it. 'You'd better hurry up about it,' he replied, 'because I want the panels in place in four weeks' time.'

I had to consider whether I needed the work and was prepared to capitulate in a game of cat and mouse or was I going to fight him. In the end, I decided I would capitulate and after another fractured telephone conversation I let him have the discount he had insisted upon. Sneakily, however, I knew I could simplify the finished artwork by tailoring it to fit the price I had in mind without him knowing and thus make up for most of the financial shortfall.

A week after the refurbished club had opened, Nardo's manager arrived in my studio to pay me. When I asked him if his boss was happy with the finished artwork, he said he didn't know, but he thought he must be, otherwise he wouldn't have paid me. In my mind's eye I could picture Nardo in his newly adorned night; this improbable little grey man, a permanent acrid expression on his face, standing in a venue that is supposed to sell happiness. When I told his manager to remind his boss that I'd be along shortly to take up the clause in our discount agreement and that I'd decided to forsake a full-blown sex session to take Nicola to dinner in his restaurant, he gave out a single and prolonged 'haaaaa!' When I looked at him for an explanation, he said, 'that's what he says to all his contractors, but he doesn't mean it. It's just his way of manipulating a deal.'

4 Winter Food

In winter, a forlorn cold settles upon northern Italy and all but puts the country into sleep mode. For me, keeping warm is an effort. In my work, paint refuses to dry and on a personal level, I need something to look forward to, to keep my spirits up. Sometimes such an event comes around in good time. One dreary January morning in piazza Roma I literally bumped into Bruno, one of our fountain-side regulars and nearly knocked him flying. He is a retired waiter, with an artificial hip and bushy, whiter-than-white hair. It was market day and he was carrying two bags of fruit and vegetables he'd just bought. After we had apologised to each other for the collision, he said it was a coincidence we had met, because he'd been looking for me. He'd organised a *mangialonga*, one of their regular gastronomic trips, where they take a bus tour around various eating establishments and wineries. There was a spare seat available on the bus, and was I interested in going? Mauro, a retired chef had dropped out because he'd had a heart murmur overnight and he would have to go to hospital for tests. The place would cost me nothing, because it had all been booked and paid for weeks ago. He then asked me if I liked eating birds. I presumed he meant poultry, but he said he didn't have time to explain because he was in a rush and could he have my decision right there and then, or he'd find somebody else. If I wanted to go, I had to be in the piazza at seven-thirty on the dot the following morning. I'd been on several of these excursions and I knew what to expect so I said 'yes' immediately.

Although I didn't know where we were going or anything else about the outing, I knew from previous experiences of such trips that the food is always delicious, so I would always be one of the first in line. Next morning I thought I was the first to arrive in the piazza, but then I saw Bruno, beckoning to me from the door of the Bar Doge.

When I arrived at the bar, I discovered that the rest of the group were having a breakfast *caffè-corretto* - coffee with a shot of Cognac, which everyone agrees sets you up for the morning. Half an hour later, when everybody felt they were set up, we piled into the minibus. Once inside, Bruno told me about the history of this annual bash. He and eight of his mates meet up with a group of four others with whom they had done their national service in the 1960s. They always go to the same restaurant in Brescia at the same time of year. Five of those who were setting out were regulars around the fountain, but although I recognised the other four, I didn't know their names. I was introduced to them and they told me that, besides doing their National Service together, they had all been at school together and at some time or other had worked in the restaurant business or the catering trade.

If you drive directly from Argegno to Brescia it takes around two hours, but this group had a couple of diversions planned before lunchtime. The first was to Saronno, a town a few kilometres short of Milan, and it was to visit one of their old contacts. He had a warehouse stacked to its wooden rafters with salume - cured hams, huge salami, spicy sausages and there were shoulders of *pancetta affumicata* (smoked bacon) hanging from steel hooks for as far as you could see. The aroma was mouth-watering. We left there an hour later, having sampled an unlimited supply, accompanied by wine, but we didn't go far, because we had an extra passenger to pick up who was a baker. To keep us from starving to death as we waited for him, he told our driver park the van around the back of his bakery, so we could sample a vast black cherry gateau his wife had laid on. This we washed down with a very decent eight-year-old Manzocco. Around mid-day, somewhere on the outskirts of Brescia, we pulled into the car park of the restaurant we'd been making for. Here we met up with only three of the other four old soldiers.

But we were not about to eat domestic farm birds as I had thought, but *lo spiedo Bresciano*: migrating songbirds of Brescia. Although they turned out to be delicious, morally they nearly choked me when I learnt afterwards about how these birds, which were once the food of poor country folk and are now an expensive delicacy were caught. Until the nineteenth century, any poachers were mutilated if caught trying to provide meat for their families, because the ruling nobility forbade the peasants to hunt for anything larger than a bird. However, they were allowed to go after these small songbirds, which the nobility didn't want. These days the birds are shot as they pass over Brescia every November by large parties of guns and are caught in huge nets as they fall. Once a matter of survival for the poor, these birds today are shot purely for gratification.

After they've been cleaned and plucked, they are rolled in slivers of pork, roasted on skewers and served on large, white dinner plates. We were given twelve each, arranged with their heads hanging over the edge of the plate with their feet meeting in the centre, like the figures on a clock face. My neighbour, Vittorio, showed me how to eat them. He took hold of one of the bird's heads, then placed the whole of the bird, except for its head, in his mouth, clenched his teeth around it and drew all the flesh off the skeleton as he pulled it from his mouth. One bird was one mouthful. He told me to chew it carefully, because although all the shot is supposed to have been removed before cooking, a piece could have been missed and I could break a tooth on it.

While we were dining, Aldo, the fourth old soldier arrived. He was late, because on his way he'd stopped his car at the side of the road to have a leak, only to be spotted by a couple of police officers in a patrol car. They escorted him to the police station, where they cautioned him for fouling the pavement. Poor Aldo, it really wasn't his day, because after only two mouthfuls of the birds we had left him, he choked on their fine bones and we thought he was going to have a heart attack. For some minutes, there was pandemonium as several people tried pouring water down his throat and furiously patting his back, but this didn't work. Someone suggested we lay him face down on the restaurant floor and stamped on his back. That didn't work either and so the owner of the restaurant hurriedly dialled 132 for the *Croce Rosso* (the Red Cross), who took him away and evidently saved his life.

After the remains of the songbirds had been cleared away, and minus Aldo we had *brofadei* (broth), *osso buco con sedano e cuore di funghi* (braised veal shanks with chopped celery and sliced mushrooms) followed by Taleggio cheese. For desert we were served *gelato stracciatella* (ice-cream with chocolate chips) and to finish, a *caffè* with an *amaro* (liqueur).

Our next venue was in another part of Brescia, where a wine trade festival was in full swing. It was housed in a large marquee, and on offer were some of the best Italian wines money can buy. Although this was a trade event, where wine producers and merchants presented their wares to the catering, hotel and bar trade, none of our group bought anything. Because they were all retired, they no longer had to worry about tempting their customers' palates. Instead, they did a lot of sampling and a lot of talking about what they were sampling to their once-upon-a-time suppliers, as well as partaking in the various plates of foodstuffs they provided. We left the marquee around seven o'clock in the evening with a stack of freebies under our arms, arriving back in Argegno, fourteen hours after we set off and somewhat the worse for wear.

~~~

A week after the minibus outing I saw a poster in the newsagent's window, advertising a coach-trip to celebrate the end of the rice harvest. This was to take place at a restaurant near to Novara in the region of Piemonte. It was the time of year for gastronomic excursions, when the opportunity to feast excessively for next to nothing is on offer and I was in the mood for more experimental cuisine. Included in the price of the trip was a tour of the paddy fields, followed by a visit to a working rice farm and museum in Vercelli for a short lecture about the history of rice growing in Italy. The trip was arranged, as most of them are, for a weekday. As Nicola worked in Milan during the week she kept missing out on these wonderful excursions, so I persuaded her to take a day off so she could come along too. The next day I booked two tickets for the trip. Had Nicola known what we were in for, she would have preferred to go to work instead.

I was surprised to discover not only that rice was grown in Italy at all, and in such large quantities and varieties, but that the farms in the valley export sixty per cent of what they harvest. According to the farmer in Vercelli, rice growing took off in Italy in the fifteenth century. The Po Valley was found to be one of a few places in Europe with a suitably warm temperature, a vast area of flat land and a plentiful supply of water from the nearby mountains. The first records of rice being grown on the Vercelli farm date back to 1427 and the farmer informed us that Japonica varieties of rice, such as Carnaroli, Arborio, Vialone Nano, Balado and Ballila grow best and are particularly suited for making risotto. Carnaroli, one of the specialities of northern Italy is considered the king of the risotto varieties because it is the creamiest. Until the advent of special machinery in the 1960s, rice production, including the planting, weeding and harvesting was all done by hand, by thousands of women. Rice can be grown in dry fields, but most of the rice grown in Italy is produced using the paddy field system, because the water prevents weeds from overwhelming the rice, protects the seeds from frost in the early spring and shields the young crop from excessive heat in the summer. There can still be problems with aquatic weeds, but to minimise this the rice is grown in paddy fields for two years, then, using an impressive irrigation system, a farmer will drain his fields and plant barley and soya for a year. Then the fields are flooded once again for rice production.

Along with the annual rice crop, Italian farmers profit from a secondary income without having to do much to earn it. After the rice yield has been collected, dried and milled and enough stored to satisfy their own appetites and that of the wide domestic and export markets, six million frogs that had been living amongst the rice plants in the flooded fields are rounded up, killed, cleaned and packed for export.

After the tour of the farm, the next stop was the one that everyone on the trip had been waiting for, *le persone che amano il riso a la rana*, (the feast day for enthusiasts of rice with frog). Neither Nicola nor I could call ourselves enthusiasts but we had come along in case we could be in the future. I had eaten frogs' legs in Normandy a few years earlier and I remembered enjoying them. I was told before I tried them that they were like chicken breast in texture, which they were but not in taste. So, here we were, arriving at the restaurant bang on twelve thirty, and it was jam-packed. Space had been reserved for our coach party of forty-two, so we joined the other hundred and thirty expectant souls already seated at long tables with benches. No sooner had we sat down than a myriad of open wine bottles were placed in front of us on a starched white tablecloth, then the cutlery with serviettes, glasses and water in jugs arrived, along with grissini and baskets of panini.

Next came the *antipasto*, the starter. When I enter a restaurant, I find it helps to sniff the interior, because it can act as an appetiser, but I have to say that this one smelt rather strange. It was what I can only describe as a dirty smell, as if the place hadn't been cleaned for a while. I felt I wanted to open the windows and blow away stale air. But the restaurant didn't look dirty; quite the opposite, so I dismissed my doubts. That was until the antipasto, *frittata a la rana* arrived, the plates passed over our heads from the kitchen. It was the first omelette I'd ever seen that was a pale grey in colour with black specks mixed into it. This was the source of the unpleasant smell. We were told that the black specks were pieces of minced frog. It was easy to eat because it was very thin, so, along with everybody else I ate it, in three mouthfuls, but I didn't enjoy it. Nicola, I noticed, picked up a minuscule amount of it on the edge of her fork, then after a tentative taste left the rest of it untouched. Some of our group asked for seconds, then thirds. We didn't.

The next course, *il primo piatto* was risotto with frog. This was the speciality that folk had travelled long distances to try and they looked very excited about it. This time, instead of the plates being passed over our heads they were filled from a convoy of trolleys, each one holding a huge tureen. The risotto was white and creamy, looking as it should be, but once again there was that odd, dirty smell along with it. Closely inspecting my bowlful I could see a tiny amputated hand, if not two resting on top of the rice and an eye peering up at me. I was timid about tasting the mixture, so before I did I removed the eye. I thought perhaps I'd been unfortunate and that I should complain to the waiter about having an identifiable piece of dead frog staring at me, but because everybody else was by now tucking into theirs and appearing to relish each mouthful (there was even applause from a couple of the tables), I thought it best not to spoil the party. With some difficulty, I did manage to swallow two spoonfuls of rice that looked to be clear of frog, but then I gave up. It tasted like it smelt: dirty. Then it dawned on me what the smell reminded me of. When I was a lad and I used to go fishing for sticklebacks in a ditch near my home in Formby on Merseyside. On several occasions I fell in and swallowed some of the water. Po Valley frog has the same iron taste as the ditch water I had swallowed. Once again Nicola left hers untouched, preferring instead to fill up on the local red wine.

The main course, *il piatto secondo* consisted of roast frog with roast potatoes, roast carrots and roast zucchini. This plate revealed what the frogs were like whole: little, trussed up dark green things, prepared for the oven like miniature chickens, with their heads and feet removed and their back legs tucked under their front legs. Once again they smelt and tasted nasty. After I'd tasted the one I had in front of me I left it alone. I ate the vegetables, which I assumed had been roasted separately from the frogs, because they didn't taste tainted. When Nicola saw what had been placed in front of her, she didn't even bother picking up her knife and fork.

But when I asked a passing waitress if she had anything to eat that didn't contain frog, every head in the restaurant appeared to turn towards me. It was as if they had all heard my request at the same time, or perhaps word had spread along the tables about what I had said, because they all stopped eating. Up until then the gathering had been fairly rowdy, but a perceptible silence fell over the whole room. Then, all together, the diners at the far end of the restaurant, who seemed to be having difficulty identifying who it was who had the audacity to be irreverent towards this wonderful food, rose to their feet to get a better look at me. Unfamiliar faces joined forces with the ones I knew from Argegno. All had a look of disbelief, if not of horror. Then, there was uproar in the form of jeers and sneers, followed by a lot of pointing and then laughter. Seconds after that I received their collective opinion of what they thought of me. I was classified as a failure, a novice and unmanly, and one of them shouted out, 'why are you here?'

One of our coach party, sitting opposite me took it upon himself to inform the entire clientele of the restaurant what it was they clearly did not know. He stood on his bench and shouted above the laughter, 'lui è Inglese (he's English)!' This statement seemed to allay the attention I was getting, as if it said everything they needed to know. After that was done and dusted, they settled back into their places once again to continue eating their frogs. The only dish without any frog in it was the cheese salad the waitress knocked up for us two withering Inglesi, and after that there was a wine break, followed by - wait for it - frog ice cream.

5 Claudio and some Ostriches

The following summer I put two Trompe l'Oeil paintings of traditional foodstuffs local to the Lombardy region I had done in an open art exhibition in Como. Over a complimentary glass of wine at the private view I met a fellow exhibitor, a man named Claudio. He was an outgoing character with a booming voice and a forceful personality and I took a liking to him, because he made me laugh with his wry sense of humour. He took me to see the two paintings he had on show. Both were extremely large, colourful, splashy abstracts, one primarily in yellow and the other predominantly vermilion. There didn't appear to be any subject matter involved in either of them and I got the impression that he was an enthusiastic operator rather than a painter. His technique seemed to be to throw overwhelming amounts of thick paint directly onto the canvas from tins and from some distance, because the splash marks were long, and the empty tins were in evidence as the focal point in each painting.

After a few seconds of my looking at Claudio's abstracts, he asked me what I thought of them, but it was difficult to think of anything to say that was complimentary. Privately, I wasn't keen on them, partly because I don't like abstract paintings, especially splashy ones, because they all look the same regardless of who has done the splashing and partly because I fail to appreciate them as fine art. They are, on the other hand, acceptable as decorative pieces for a room that needs some colour, or as designs for dress fabric and the like. Although I felt like telling him I'd seen monkeys in zoos come up with similar results, I didn't, but for the sake of saying something complimentary I said that I admired his bold use of thick paint and intense colour.

He told me he believed that his work contained great technical ability, and he set about trying to impress upon me what a painting of true emotion contains by saying that he paints best when he is angry or in love, and to demonstrate his feelings he finds the easiest way is to put them down in paint form. He added that the two on display were some of the best paintings he had ever done. According to the catalogue, the yellow one was entitled "The Inconsistency of Refutation", and the red one was about "The Supremacy of Corporeal Reality." He asked to see the two paintings I had on display, so we went to view them. I didn't ask him what he thought of them, but he must have been impressed because he said, 'I can market you.'

Over a period of a few months I got to know Claudio a little better, mainly through some heavy social sessions in his favourite Mexican Tequila bar in Milan. It was in a dingy area of the city where bohemians hang out, where he liked to live the life of "the artist" or what he imagined it was like. He believed this involved a lot of drinking, talking philosophically about art to whoever would listen, and being wayward. When he socialised he said he liked to be around artists, and as the bar was close to the Accademia di Brera, the state-run academy of fine arts, he had the opportunity to do so, because artists and students frequented it. The only problem was that Claudio wasn't an artist, although he told everybody he was. He was appreciative and enthusiastic about art and all that surrounds it, and he entered his paintings in just about every open art exhibition he saw advertised, but the honest truth was that because he hadn't been trained, I can't think that he would have been able to draw a straight line if his life had depended on it. For a short while he had me fooled, because he talked as if he was in possession of the fundamental requirements any artist worth his salt has to have to make a living. And as I got to know him better I found out that when it came to selling his splashy abstracts he was highly successful at it. Therefore, although I had become suspicious of his credibility as a painter I was interested to find out about his marketing side and I soon found out.

It was his gift of the gab that earned him some wealthy patrons, all of whom happened to work for Olivetti. He had gained them, and some of their wealth by inviting them to the Mexican bar after work and during happy hour (which, in his presence could last until closing time) where he would pour Tequila Margaritas or Mescal down their necks until they didn't know what they were doing, and then he'd charge them top dollar for the privilege of owning "a Claudio".

Although Claudio looked like a genuine artist, in the sense that his appearance was carefree and paint-splashed, he was in fact a bookkeeper for Olivetti. Splashing paint around was a hobby he wanted to turn into a profession because, he said, he detested being a bookkeeper. Claudio was physically big, with most of his size situated around his waist and thighs. His face and chest were dominated by a long, substantial black beard and he had a pair of round, black-rimmed John Lennon style spectacles that he would perch on the end of his nose. I often considered what the real Claudio might look like underneath the façade. He always wore a black T-shirt and heavy black cotton trousers, which were in contrast to his ever-colourful personality. He never wore a sweater, because he said he wore one once and caught a chill. I think his blubber must have kept him warm in the winter, because the only other clothing I ever saw him wear, even on the coldest of days was a black jacket, or if he was in his studio in Como, a paint-stained smock and a black beret. He maintained he was a contemporary artist and he believed that what he produced was progressive, twenty-first century art. I didn't argue with his illusion. Anybody with even a basic knowledge of art history knows that splashy abstraction has been around since the nineteen thirties and although Claudio believed he had moved abstraction on, he hadn't. And although he said he was a person of today, what he wore when he splashing paint around was a cliché of the outfit worn by a Victorian artist. The first time I saw him in his painting garb I couldn't help smirking: no modern day artist wears a smock and a beret unless they are attending a fancy dress party.

~~~

I hadn't seen or heard from Claudio for a couple of months, so I assumed the novelty of our acquaintanceship had come to an end, but he unexpectedly walked into our villa one Saturday afternoon and greeted me like a brother. It was the first time Nicola had met him, so to get to know him better she invited him to stay for dinner. During and after the meal a lot of wine was consumed, but I noticed it was he who carried on drinking long after we'd had enough.

Besides drinking, there was a reason for his visit, which was to tell me he had "marketed" me. One of his contacts, who happened to be a director of Olivetti wanted a Trompe l'Oeil mural painting in his lounge. He was, Claudio said, a contact with a lot of money to spend on his home and he was sure we could work together to take some of it off him. When he said the phrase 'work together', I presumed he meant that I would be the artist doing the painting and he would be acting as my agent and he would want a percentage for finding the job. Yes, he did want an agent's percentage, but he also wanted to be my assistant so he could learn how to paint a mural. I asked him how he intended going about this, because firstly, he wasn't a representational painter and secondly, as he had a full time job with Olivetti in Milan, I wanted to know how was he going to make himself available to be my assistant? He replied that the job was in the old Roman city of Pavia and he was planning on taking two weeks holiday to do it. At this early stage of our working relationship I agreed to give him the benefit of the doubt about his painting ability and experience, so we shook hands on division of the fee; sixty-forty in my favour. The next day we drove to Pavia for a meeting with the client in his magnificent Liberty-style home, where we sat overlooking the city to discuss the design, the fee and the living arrangements. I was impressed with Claudio's business acumen and he got a good deal out of the client, with a nice *anticipo* (an advance payment). He also got the client to agree to pay for us to stay in an *agriturismo* (farmhouse lodging) for the estimated time the job was going to take. The design I came up with for the mural was as if a hole had been knocked through the clients lounge wall and the viewer could see the handsome old city in the distance. The other walls were to be colour-washed to give an aged effect. The client liked it, but I estimated that it would take four working weeks to do the job and not the two Claudio intended taking off from bookkeeping.

Two weeks later, having persuaded Claudio to replace his smock and beret with a pair of white overalls, we started on the Pavia project. It was one I shall never forget, for reasons that came to light after we had spent a few hours setting up. As we unloaded the paint, materials and aluminium ladders required for the job from my car, covered the client's lounge floor with plastic sheeting, spread thick cotton dust sheets over the furniture and masked the electrical fittings, I discovered that Claudio's attitude towards the job wasn't the same as mine. We were almost at the end of our first day of working together when he became impatient and told me, 'I thought we had come here to paint a mural, not to be labourers!'

I told him that we first had to protect the room from the possibility of paint spillage. Then, the following day, we had to apply the colour-washes to the walls. Only then could we start painting the mural. I could tell from Claudio's reaction that this wasn't really what he wanted to hear, because his right eye had started to twitch. This was not that noticeable to somebody who didn't know him, and it was usually the start of a lot of sighing and blaspheming.

The next day I mixed up four large buckets of paint in several light terra cotta shades for the colour-washing. We then placed the ladders in position and I showed him how to apply the first colour-wash. I told him I would follow on with the second colour-wash, applying it whilst his wash was still damp. I then handed him a full bucket of paint and wished him the best of luck. He seemed to be coping with it, because to do a successful colour-wash you need to cover a large area quickly using large brushes and large brush strokes, applying thin glazes, one on top of the other while the previous one is still damp, at the same time being careful not to let the wash run downwards. The darkest tone goes on first, followed by the three lighter tones, finishing with the lightest one. It's a splashy process, and I knew Claudio had plenty of practice at that. We were getting along swimmingly until we were into the afternoon session, when he suddenly laid his brush down and stopped work. 'I've had enough of this,' he said. 'This is going to take days to finish and I want to start painting the mural.'

I told him that the colour-washing should take the two of us four days to complete. At this, he pouted like a child and said, 'as from now, I've got eight and a half days' holiday left. I thought we would be starting the mural first and you would be doing the paint effects after I've left.'

When we had finished a day's work, we went to our *agriturismo* accommodation. This type of accommodation is found on a farm or a smallholding and gets its name from a combination of two words; *agricoltura* (agriculture) and *turismo* (tourism). They came about in the 1950s as farming in Italy became less profitable and many farmers abandoned their farms in search of work in the towns and cities. To keep the countryside alive, the government stepped in with subsidies for farmers who were willing to switch over to *agriturismi*. To qualify for an agriturismo subsidy a farm still had to operate as a farm. Some were arable farms, others were fruit and vegetable producers and others were dairy farms or reared animals for meat. The agriturismo the client had booked us into was ten kilometres from the centre of Pavia. Originally it had been large and they used to rear pigs, cattle and chickens, but now they reared *struzzi* - ostriches. In recent years the largest portion of the land had been converted into a riding stable and the land used for public equestrian events, exercising horses and for grazing. The yard nearest to the farmhouse was now a guest car park. Near to it were the four two-hundred-year old brick-built barns that were used for guest accommodation, which had been tastefully transformed into twenty spacious bedrooms, with en-suite bathrooms, balconies and terraces. They were accessed through an archway that led into a courtyard. At the other side of the courtyard was the farmhouse, which was also large, with the farmer's residence upstairs. The downstairs had been converted into a kitchen and dining room. A glass conservatory had been added to the south side, which was used as a dining area for up to sixty people.

An agriturismo is similar in some ways to an English bed and breakfast, except they can also do full board if required. Because they are converted farms they are well away from any amenities, so it is essential to have a car to get to them. This means that in the evenings, unless you travel to the nearest town, there isn't much to do except talk to fellow residents. These will usually be Italian, because although foreign tourists are becoming more aware of agriturismi, they are most popular with Italians.

Our first night at the struzzi farm was an eye-opening experience for me, because after we had booked in and had a splendid dinner, I discovered a side to Claudio I had suspected, but hadn't yet seen. The social Claudio was a different animal from the working one and now there was a safety margin of a hundred kilometres between him and his wife he intended to make the most of it. He couldn't wait to visit Pavia to scout for a woman. He'd heard there was a Mexican bar there that would provide what he was looking for, so off he went to find it while I stayed at the agriturismo. A few hours later, the black-clad beast returned empty-handed, because although he found the bar, he discovered it was closed on Mondays. This was a relief, because I'd had this image of him rocking up in the middle of the night with a woman and I dreaded the embarrassment it might cause the owners. Subtlety and sobriety weren't in Claudio's make-up and when I talked to him about being discreet, he gave me a glowering look and sloped off to bed.

The following night was a repeat of the previous one, only this time he must have arrived back late, because he didn't come down for breakfast. I banged on his bedroom door several times, but there was no reply and the only way I could wake him was by calling his cell phone. This meant that we arrived at the client's house two hours later than I had wanted and almost immediately Claudio and I had some heated words. He was reluctant to climb up the ladder to continue the colour-washing because he said he was tired. Fortunately, the room we were working in was out of the family's earshot and so I told him that before we went any further I wanted some assurances from him.

If he wanted to visit the various watering holes in Pavia, it was OK by me as long as he remembered his responsibilities to the client and to me and he put in a full day's work. As it was, he would struggle to stay the course, because he wasn't anywhere near fit enough for what was hard, physical work.

During day four, the day before we were due to start the mural, he was so tired from his late night excursions that he said he was going to stay in that night so he would be fresh for the morning. However, when we got back to the struzzi farm that evening, we discovered it was full of gay Italian pilots and flight attendants, who were attending a safety training conference at the nearby airport and were staying in our agriturismo. At the dining table that night and for most of the following week we were surrounded by handsome, sun tanned men in white short sleeved shirts with gold braid epaulets, who gave us the eye remorselessly. It was oppressive, and it made me understand how women must feel when they get pestered by men they would rather not know. It was easy to tell the difference between the pilots and the cabin crew, because the pilots had more pips on their epaulets and the cabin crew had whiter teeth. Either there had been a cheap offer for teeth whitening, or it had become mandatory for anyone pushing a trolley up the isle of a passenger aircraft, because I found myself staring across the dinner table at rows of pearly-white teeth. Like me, Claudio wanted to get away from these men as soon as he could. Immediately dinner was over he forgot he was tired and we went to a bowling alley in the centre of Pavia, hoping that everybody else would be in bed when we returned.

Day five arrived, the moment Claudio had been busting for. We could start mapping out the mural from the design, but after only an hour he received a phone call from his wife, telling him his mother had died in the night and he had to go back to Como to organise the funeral. He left immediately and I didn't see or hear from him again for ten days, in which time I had made good progress with the mural. Naturally, he was still upset by the loss of his parent but it seemed to have had a calming effect on him and he seemed much fresher than when I last saw him. He told me that he'd taken an extra week off for compassionate reasons and now he would be able to work on the mural. until it was finished.

By this time the aircrew had left the farm, so he, like me Claudio was content to stay in at night and feed his face on the various delightful dishes of ostrich meat and eggs the farmer's wife placed in front of us. Ostriches were often the centre of conversation around the dinner table during our stay at the farm. One evening we went to see the ostrich pens to admire the birds, where the farmer informed us that although he served the meat in the restaurant, he sold most of it and most of the eggs to a wholesaler. He also sold the skins to people who made high quality leather goods, and the feathers went to be made into boas and dusters. Although ostriches cannot fly for great distances, they can flap their wings sufficiently enough to get out of their pen. We were advised that if we saw any of them wandering around the farmyard not to touch them, because they could kick hard enough to break a leg.

On the menu was a choice of ostrich meat in all its forms. Because it is low in fat and cholesterol it is supposed to be far healthier than beef or pork and Claudio and I found we preferred its flavour. I thought it would be similar to chicken or turkey in taste, but surprisingly it is dark, and it is cooked in the same way as any other red meat. Nevertheless, it still seemed odd eating ostrich salami, ostrich burgers and ostrich fillet steaks for the first time, or ostrich mince in a Bolognese sauce. On another night we ate it cured, in carpaccio form on crackers for a starter, then an ostrich leg roast, with home grown vegetables. But the most amusing of all was eating ostrich eggs. An ostrich egg weighs over a kilo, which is twenty times heavier than a hen's egg and is enough to feed six people. A single egg takes an hour and a half to boil and fifteen minutes to fry. I shall never forget the night when Claudio and I came back to the farm after a hard day's work feeling particularly hungry when the farmer's wife placed a silver tureen on the dining table, saying it was just for us two. Claudio lifted the lid and there, sitting on a bed of lettuce was the Italian equivalent of an enormous deep-fried scotch egg. We struggled to eat half of it.

We finished the mural on day twenty as I'd predicted, but not as a team. Claudio learnt what he wanted to know by sitting in an armchair watching me work, because that was where I'd told him to stay. All the sections of the mural I'd given him to do he'd botched up and I had to re-do them, so making him sit in an armchair out of harm's way was the best thing to do. For him, the one constructive thing to come out of our relationship was that he undoubtedly realised that if he wanted to paint representatively, he had better go to night classes to study drawing. And for a long time.

Since the Pavia fiasco, Claudio has telephoned me a couple of times to invite me to his favourite tequila bar, but I have made excuses not to go. He has never mentioned the mural event, nor has he suggested any further "partnership arrangements". If he had, I would have made an excuse not to get involved in them either.

6 Val d'Intelvi

Argegno village is 152 metres (500 feet) above sea level, just above the level of Lake Como. The Val d'Intelvi (The Intelvi Valley) is a mountainous agricultural area that begins behind the village and rises for a further 1,300 metres. It was inhabited long before the Romans arrived, and towards the end of the seventeenth century it became famous for the Intelvi masters, who were stone masons and craftsmen in *scagliola* (gesso work, from the Italian *scaglia*, meaning "chips"). The high quality of the work was out of proportion to such a comparatively tiny area and the masters' decorative artwork adorns some of Italy's finest cathedrals, churches and palaces.

Scagliola is a little known technique used to decorate stucco columns, sculptures and other architectural elements and it became a substitute for costly marble. It can also be used to decorate picture frames, mirror surrounds and other furnishings. Although examples of scagliola are comparatively hard to find outside the Intelvi region, and for that matter, Italy in general, there are some examples of the technique to be found abroad. At one time there were many studios in the valley producing scagliola, but now there is only one small studio remaining. However, these days the studio mainly restores the work of the original craftsmen, which is often found many miles from the Val d'Intelvi.

I discovered scagliola when I painted a large mural for a client, a local farmer who lived at the very top of the Intelvi valley. He told me all about the artistic heritage of the area and showed me examples in the local churches. Even though I had heard of it, I was surprised to discover what it actually was, because I'd always presumed it to be inlaid marble veneer. I visited some of the Intelvi churches where I was told I could see some excellent examples of the work and in one, the priest asked me why I was examining his altar so closely. I told him I was fascinated by the technique, and although it had been around for three hundred years, I didn't know what it was until my client had introduced me to it. The priest then told me about its history and its importance to the region. From then on I became an admirer.

Apart from the artwork, Intelvi is also famous because it is an area where visitors can experience what life was like in Italy a century or so ago. It is more popular with Italians than with foreign tourists, because although tourists will know of Lake Como and how it dominates the area, few will explore the Intelvi Valley, because it isn't publicised very much. Nicola and I had heard about the area from some of our older neighbours when we lived in Moltrasio. They had said we should visit it before the way of life there disappears completely. However, we never had the opportunity until we moved to Argegno, which came when I went to the paint shop in Como where I buy my materials, and the owner handed me a piece of paper. On it was the phone number of a farmer from Intelvi, and a request to contact him, because he wanted me to paint some artwork for him.

The next day I met the farmer, Signor Daniele for aperitivi before lunch in a bar in the tiny village of Verna, which is halfway up a mountain. We drank a little too much Martini rosso, which was one of his favourite tipples, then went to his house in Ramponio for lunch to try another of his favourites, his homemade Barbera wine. Ramponio is the highest village in the Intelvi and it sits on a plateau known as *il balcone d'Italia* (the balcony of Italy) above a point where the mountain road dips down into Switzerland and it offers a stunning view of Lake Lugano.

I would go on to work for Daniele for three weeks during a blisteringly hot June and he proved to be from a different mould, a farmer in the traditional sense. He had a widespread of land, a herd of cows, dozens of goats, a hundred rabbits, the same number of free-range hens and a boar he was fattening for Christmas, but he was most noted in the area as a donkey breeder. It was plain for anybody to see that Daniele had a passion for donkeys, which he found fascinating, even beautiful. He kept fifteen of them as a nucleus for breeding and he said he had so many orders for donkeys from other farmers in the area, and his two donkey stallions were worked hard, covering the mares of other farmers. Most, but not all of Daniele's donkeys were bought to keep a good deal of the Intelvi grass under control. 'One single donkey,' he told me, 'will eat at least two acres of knee-high grass per year, and apart from a few hours sleep they will eat during the night as well if they got the chance.'

Daniele also sold his donkeys for meat, because the locals like to eat it with their polenta. He also bred goats, which he said also do a good job keeping the grass down, but most farmers prefer donkeys, because although nanny goat will give milk, they tend to jump fences and unless they are tethered they wander off, which means a farmer has to keep moving them once they have devoured all the grass within the range of the rope. Donkeys, on the other hand can be put in a field with a shelter and then left until they've eaten all the grass.

Daniele's kind nature was written on his face. He was a

tall, well built man, more sinewy than muscled, without a kilogram of excess fat on him and bronzed through a life spent out of doors. He had huge, rough, permanently soiled hands that reminded me of the root vegetables he might have just pulled up. When he shook my hand, which was often, dust would fall from his own hands. Everybody I met while working in the Intelvi knew Daniele. They liked him and respected him because of his experience in the ways of country life. He was a fixture in the community; if anybody arrived to see him and he wasn't around his farm, all they had to do was search his fields to find him. He would work from five thirty in the morning until dark, seven days a week. His work was his life and there was plenty of it to do. I asked him how many hours a week he worked. He put his hand to his chin, waited a few seconds and then said that he'd never thought about it. It was like asking somebody how many times a day they breathed. He even ate his meals outside. He certainly drank outside - and plenty of it - and it was always around his stone table. This was a huge piece of granite that had been placed under a vine-covered pergola half way down his garden. It must have taken a dozen men to lift into position. His life seemed to be conducted around this table. It was his resting place, his meal table, his social centre and the place he did business. He had a store cupboard built into the rock behind it to keep his wine at a constant temperature for when the business of the day was concluded, when he would celebrate by cracking open yet another two-litre bottle. I asked him how much he drank per week. He put his hand to his chin once more and said again that he'd never thought about it.

He was a man who knew how to survive and survive well in a place without mains water or gas. He knew how to plough land. He knew when to sow seeds and when and how to harvest. He knew how to breed animals, when and how to slaughter them and how to cook them. He knew how to make wine. He knew how to maintain and handle heavy machinery. He knew how to build dry stone walls and how to put up fencing. He knew how to store water and he knew how to make money. The only thing he admitted to not knowing was how to draw and paint and if it had been possible to swap skills with him I would have done so gladly. He proved to be a fantastic guy, far preferable in every way to some of the clientele I was familiar with and I gladly gave him a large *sconto* without him having to ask for one. We took to each other from the day we met and he became an instant friend.

Daniele was sixty-two when he began building a dream home for his wife. Before that, they had lived in a tiny, two-up two-down traditional stone house since they married, thirty-seven years before. In many ways, though an "all mod cons" house seemed to be inconsistent with the way he was, because he seemed to be from an earlier century.

When I lived in the UK I had painted murals in properties owned by some of the world's wealthiest and most famous celebrities, and when I moved to Italy I worked for the Como architects' wealthy clients, but I had never worked for a farmer before. Daniele was in the process of finishing the house when he decided he wanted a mural painted along the north-facing exterior wall. He wanted something in a contemporary style, which I enjoy painting, which was an unusual request from an Italian. They tend to go for more traditional subjects, so I don't get asked to paint them very often, and certainly not in a village that still celebrates a life that existed long before any of us were born. Although I paint in the representative manner of the seventeenth century Italian masters, I like to paint subjects of today rather than of yesteryear and I was interested to see if Daniele would hesitate at an idea I'd just had. He showed me the wall at the side of his house, which he had already prepared in an off-white exterior paint, but he didn't have any ideas of what he wanted painting on it.

'No worries,' I said. 'I have one.' It had hit me immediately I saw his donkeys. It had to be a mural about donkeys.

He thought I was joking, but I wasn't. I'd brought my camera, so I asked him if he'd let me into two of the paddocks he had. In the first one I photographed his two stallions and in the other, two pregnant mares. We then went and found the rest of the mares in the fields, half hidden by knee-high grass. I then did a quick sketch to show him what I had in mind. When we returned to the house, we found his friend Renzo sitting at the stone table so Daniele asked him what he thought. Renzo liked the idea, so a week later I started painting Daniele's fifteen donkeys, including a heavily pregnant mare, full size.

It takes forty-five minutes to drive from Argegno to Ramponio along a steep winding, twelve kilometre long road and the car's engine was always hot when I arrived. But I didn't mind that, because every day was like a working holiday. There was none of the pressure exerted by cantankerous clients or measly architects who constantly threatened me with penalty clauses if the work didn't look as if it was going to be finished on time. If Daniele was around, instead of getting the whip out, he'd get the bottle out and within an hour of my starting to paint he would insist I join him and generally one or two of his friends around the table for a chat.

I never take a lunch break when I'm working. It's a habit I brought with me from the UK when time was money. Skipping lunch was essential if I wanted to beat the traffic build-up on the M25 to get back to Godalming from London each evening. Not so in the Intelvi Valley. Lunch lasted an hour and then I had to have a half hour nap on a paillasse in the barn. If I didn't, he and his friends thought I was peculiar, or even crazy. (Rush-hour traffic in the Intelvi usually consisted of an occasional tractor or a herd of sheep. Once that had been negotiated, it was case of free-wheeling down the mountain pass, all the way back to Argegno.) For lunch, Daniele's wife would bring a basket from the house, filled with salami, ham on the bone, salad, hard-boiled eggs, a home made baguette and, always a two-litre bottle of Barbera. I never expected any lunch, but Daniele would insist on my finishing work dead on mid-day to join them around the stone table.

Daniele was an honest, relaxed dependable man. He had a lifestyle that was simple, yet it required all the skill in the world to carry it out. It was based on self-sufficiency; not in the trendy sense of the term but in the real sense. If he made a mistake, then he and his family would suffer. If there were a bad harvest or a drought, he would have problems. There were no supermarkets around the corner to help out. He was an object lesson for us all but one day things did go awry on his farm. Overnight, a deer had got into his lettuces and cabbages and had eaten the lot. He said he intended to wait up that night to shoot it. At nine o'clock the next morning when I arrived, the deer was hanging from ropes in the barn, waiting to be skinned.

I felt saddened when the time came to say goodbye to Daniele and friends, and I thought that would be that in Ramponio, but he said he was having none of it. I left with a cheque, two two-litre bottles of Barbera, a pound of donkey meat sausages and an invitation for Nicola and me to attend all his *feste*. Daniele never missed an Italian public holiday. Each one was an excuse for a *festa grande*. He had a calendar pasted inside his wine cupboard with all the festa days circled in red and the next one was in two weeks' time. Nicola and I could hardly wait for it to arrive. On the menu was to be polenta mixed with four cheeses, served on a grand scale, with several racks of beef. I'd never seen a polenta pot so big and after it had been stirred constantly for three hours, a crowd of friends and relatives arrived to congregate around the stone table, ready to celebrate whatever saint's day it was. With them they'd brought *il dolce* - the dessert: tiramisu, meringata (ice cream with meringue topping and hot chocolate sauce) and pasticcini

– small pastries of all kinds.

After several feste, Nicola and I began to consider what it would be like to live in the Val d'Intelvi, because the more we visited, the more we liked it. In a way we were already living in the Intelvi, because our villa is the very first building on the road heading out of Argegno up to the Intelvi valley, but it was at the base of the mountain and it was the higher part we had begun to admire so much. We then began to wonder if we could afford a homestead with some land so we could have animals as pets. Nicola has always dreamed of having a dog, or maybe two, but since we'd been in Italy we hadn't had any suitable land to let a dog or dogs out. We'd also dreamt of owning a horse to ride, a couple of goats, some chickens, maybe a rabbit and possibly one of Daniele's donkeys, and of course more cats; in other words, a small farm, so we asked Daniele what he thought about our crazy idea.

Practicalities, Daniele said came first; could we find a suitable place that was for sale? He said it would be good to have us as neighbours and he had heard there where three places for sale nearby, and if we were serious about taking on a lot of work owning animals he would make some enquiries for us. A few days later we met him at his house and from there he took us in his 4x4 to view one of them. This had a long driveway and a lot of woodland. In fact it had twenty thousand square metres of land in all, with a spectacular view over Lake Lugano. The price was reasonable and there were plenty of out buildings for animals already in situ. The people who were selling the place were old and the husband was bed-ridden. Their son wanted to sell it so he could move his parents nearer to a town. There was no mains gas, but there was a propane tank. This is not uncommon in Italy, because half the country is built on rock and so it is difficult and expensive, if not impossible to lay pipes, especially to individual properties off the beaten track. There was electricity in the farmhouse, which was supplied by overhead cables, and there was enough wood in the surrounding woodland to keep the stove burning for decades. However, Daniele advised us not to buy it, because although everything about the place seemed ideal for us, there was no mains water. The only water supply was from rainfall, trapped in storage tanks from what ran off the roof of the house and outbuildings. He said this was common in the valley, but not advisable because if we wanted to have a lot of animals and if there was a drought it could be catastrophic. Because of climate change, there have been periods when there hasn't been any rain for months, and the people who weren't on mains water had to have it delivered by tanker, which was not cheap. It was still a place to get excited about, and for a couple of days after we had viewed it we considered buying it, but we had to listen to Daniele's advice, because he knew everything there was to know about the area. We were seeing the homestead in ideal summer conditions, but the farm was 1,400 metres (3,280 feet) above sea level and the winter snow could be deep and remain for months. Because the road to the house would only be used by us, it wouldn't be cleared of snow by the comune, so we could be totally marooned unless we paid for the services of a snowplough. Reluctantly we had to leave it.

We met Daniele a week later outside his house to see prospect number two on his list. This was a *rustico*, which was a polite way of saying that it needed a lot of work doing to it before it was habitable, which is why rustici are generally cheap to buy; buyers can end up spending more than they are worth to make them habitable. And as with a lot of *rustici* in Italy, there are strict building regulations about what we could and couldn't do to it to them. What made it nearly worth considering was that it had plenty of outbuildings and the right amount of fairly flat open grassland, including enough to grow winter feed. This would be ideal for the amount of animals we anticipated having. Its position wasn't isolated and the access road was in good condition. There wasn't any mains water, but it could have been laid on from the main road for a price, but because of the rules surrounding rustici the problem would be getting planning permission. Worst of all, the farmhouse was too small for us to live in, and although the legislation only allows for a twenty per cent enlargement of an existing building, that still would not have given us enough space. In the end we said no. We were sure we wouldn't be able to afford what it might end up costing us.

There was a third property to see and this one had everything we needed; mains facilities, the right amount of agricultural land and a farm house that was as pretty as a picture, with a wicket gate, sun-flowers and hollyhocks in the garden, climbing roses around the front door and a fully equipped stable for the horse, but the vendor wanted €300,000 for it, which was way above our budget. After that, we became hesitant about moving to a rural location, so we decided to put the homestead idea on hold. Daniele had given us an insight into what Intelvi life was all about, which was that it was a full time job. Our intention of mixing the two systems together; the modern one, where Nicola commuted to Milan and I go off to paint the homes of the wealthy and run a farmstead in the manner formulated centuries ago wasn't going to be easy to achieve, but it hasn't been forgotten about entirely.

7 Local Tittle-tattle

All the restaurants and bars in Argegno are family businesses, passed down from generation to generation. During opening hours, the whole village echoes to the sound of the diners. The present proprietors continue to rake in the money, 364 days a year, yet they appear to be bored with making money, setting their tables with a look of indifference in their eyes. Maybe they wonder why they are serving, when they are the masters. Perhaps their dilemma has come about because their restaurants are so popular they have become imprisoned within their own establishments because customers rule every hour of their lives. Their problem seems to be that they know that if they give it up, they will finish like Mario, the millionaire who sold his restaurant for more than its worth and end up like him a fish out of water, with plenty of money but no idea of what to do with it. To them, the family business is a dictator, which means they are up to their necks in the daily *sugo* of rules, contracts, bank accounts, property and washing-up, as well as fulfilling their responsibilities to themselves and to their families, past, present and future. They must not let the side down, even if it means forfeiting their own lives. Do they ever stand aside and examine the amount of the available time they have left to enjoy what they have made? I doubt it.

For the month I was working on Daniele's mural in Ramponio I hadn't been able to attend the old boys' meetings, but I must have made an impression before I left. Previously, if I hadn't attended a meeting, the next time I appeared I would receive a stiff reminder that aperitivi happens every day. This time when I arrive, instead of receiving a telling off for being absent I am given a warm welcome. It seemed they were beginning to accept that I have to make a living.

Alessandro has just been warned to look out, because his wife has been seen in the vicinity of the piazza. According to the old boys, if Alessandro's wife sees his eye wander, she can be ruthless. They wonder why he keeps her. She's what is commonly called in Italy a *rompe ballo* - a "ball-breaker", because she tries her best to ruin his fun. She watches him like a hawk and knowing what he's like behind her back, who can blame her? She can never relax, but she's stuck with him through thick and thin - probably more thin than thick. Her fiery nature means that for most of Alessandro's married life he may have felt like he has been living with a simmering volcano. Money is probably what makes her stay with him; he, like Mario, has pots of it invested in all manner of nefarious tax avoidance schemes. Maybe she is biding her time for the opportunity to cash in. In the meantime she enjoys making him squirm by sticking her nose into any sign of an illicit union he might be planning. A rich man with a history of extra marital activity has few sympathisers, who wait to see if he reaps what he has sown.

Anybody who observes the old boys will see that when they are out and about with their wives they are as good as gold. The cheek and the banter will be replaced by loving affection. Even though they have known every person sitting around since childhood, they will disregard them all.

And if one of them is seen in the village with his wife, then the rest of the boys remain distant from him, in case it upsets her. Such is the disposition of the Italian female of this generation that the male has to soothe her volatile temperament for as long as she demands. When his wife is on his arm, a glance in the wrong direction, or a word with a male friend or - heaven forbid - to ogle a young lady coming off the ferry is unthinkable. Or if he should see a slim young girl in high heels and showing a bare mid-riff, he will dismiss her as an abhorrent temptress who should be covered up and sent to a convent.

But if the Italian male can be a convivial family man, he can also be (if he gets the chance) a duplicitous playboy. If he is wealthy, then in the eyes of other males he has earned the right to be a serial adulterer and he will be admired all the more by them if he is one. Bruno, the retired waiter with the artificial hip says his mop of white hair was as black as coal when he was a handsome young stud in the days when he had women "gagging for it.". He, like Alessandro retains a reputation amongst his comrades for being a highly successful womaniser in the 1960s. He now has a part-time job as a gardener and handyman for a woman who lives on the other side of the lake. He refers to her as "that rich bitch." Unfortunately for Bruno, unless it is his day off or a weekend he often misses out on the old boys daily reunion, because he cannot leave his work until four o'clock in the afternoon. Then the ferry brings him back to Argegno. He is possibly the quietest of the bunch and he seems to be content to listen to the ramblings of the others. That is, until I come along, then he will position himself beside me and talk in graphic detail about his past conquests. I've never encouraged him to do this, but he seems to find me a captive audience for him to talk about the time he was a waiter in a series of top class restaurants and hotels in London. And it's not just Bruno that will do this, and not just in Italy. On several occasions I've been in conversation with an older man I barely know and they open up and talk about their past sexual conquests. I wonder why they do this, but hopefully not so much as to make them think I am distracted. Maybe it's the presence of a younger male that reminds them of their past, or maybe talking about sexual encounters might provide some common ground. Whatever it is, when Bruno talks to me about his past, it is always a one sided discourse and when I see him coming I know I am in for an onslaught. Why I don't make my excuses and run is because his stories are attention grabbing. They might not be true but they are intriguing.

This particular day's recollections included the time he worked in a hotel in The Strand in London. A regular customer, a wealthy, middle-aged Austrian woman kept telling him how he reminded her of her son. She would always sit alone and towards the back of the same table, which meant he was forced to lean over it to serve her, and as he did so she would run her hand up his inside leg and grope his tackle. Then in her broken accent she would deliver the same line, 'zees are rusty!' When he came to clear her table after she'd gone, he would always find a large tip underneath her plate, the equivalent of a £50 note today.

After that, he began waiting at the tables of a top class fish restaurant. A wealthy businessman who owned a sizable portion of London's rag trade would visit the restaurant every Saturday night with a group of friends. He would spend a fortune on plates of specific varieties of seafood, renowned for their properties as an aphrodisiac. The businessman, Bruno thought, was in his late seventies, but his wife was much younger and she always gave Bruno the come-on. Bruno said he ignored her advances because they were so blatant and he was afraid her husband would be upset if he were to acknowledge them. However, on the third Saturday of his employment, Bruno was called into the manager's office. The businessman was there as well and it appeared that he had arranged with the manager to have Bruno serve them on their Saturday night dinner date and that later, when they left the restaurant, he wanted Bruno to accompany them in their chauffeur-driven Rolls-Royce to their mansion in Cadogan Place where he, Bruno would have sex with his wife. Bruno only went twice, because the third time the boss expected him to return to work until the restaurant closed at two o'clock in the morning. There was no remuneration from the businessman, and Bruno's boss implied that a few hours off work during the busiest time of the week to spend time with a highly desirable woman was recompense enough. With that, Bruno refused to go any more, and for his disobedience he was promptly sacked.

Bruno can reel off volumes of this stuff, and whether it's a load of garbage or not I will never know, but the credible way he tells his stories gives the impression that they are true. When I mentioned the protection at work regulations for employees receiving harassment at work, he said that it all took place fifty years ago and if protection for a foreigner working illegally in Britain existed in those days, he never knew about it. He also told me about lots of other curious situations he'd found himself in as a hotel waiter, and it would seem to be that when he was on room service it was a regular occurrence to find a naked woman laying on the top of her bed, giving him the come-on. Another time, he told me the story about a famous American TV actor of the 1960s. Once again Bruno was on room service in a London hotel and one evening when he brought champagne to the actor's room, he found him sitting in an upright chair in the centre of the room stark naked, with a Spanish guitar placed across his lap. To Bruno's surprise, the actor then slid the guitar to one side revealing an enormous erection. Bruno said he dumped the champagne on a side table and fled the room.

The following day, I was daydreaming by the fountain when I was collared by Guido. Guido frightens the daylights out of me and, I should imagine, a fair proportion of the local motorists as well. He tells me he is half blind, but he rides around on a motor scooter. Fortunately he lives no further than three kilometres away from the village centre and his scooter is small, so it doesn't go very fast. Nevertheless, it beggars belief how, up until now he hasn't hit anyone or another vehicle. The old boys say he rides on autopilot. To make things worse, Guido doesn't hear too well, and since there has been a new law requiring motorcyclists in Italy to wear crash helmets, he now hears nothing at all as he rides his scooter. He told me a story that I thought was funny, (although he couldn't see the humour in it), of the days when he was a member of Como cycling club. One year the club decided to enter him in a time trial, hoping he would win a big trophy for them. It was in the days before cars or scooters were as common as they are now, so he had to cycle the forty kilometres from Argegno to the outskirts of Como to join the tournament. Sadly he never won it because by the time he got to the starting point he was too tired to finish the race.

But Guido didn't want to talk about cycling, scooters, blindness or his lack of hearing. He wanted to talk about his prostate gland operation. I've noticed that when he starts talking about his ailments it encourages a competition amongst the others to find out who is suffering the most serious health problem. According to Guido it is most definitely himself. Four years ago, he started to have difficulty urinating. This grew steadily worse, until one day when he was busting to go for a leak, nothing came out. The hospital told him there was a four-month waiting list for the operation to remove the enlarged gland that was stopping him from peeing and in the meantime they fitted a tube through his penis and into his bladder, with a spigot on the end so he could turn it on and off to relieve himself. They then put him on antibiotics to alleviate the threat of infection from the tube and duly forgot about him. Four months later, when he chivvied them about the date of his operation the hospital couldn't find any record of him or his previous treatment, so he had to go to the bottom of the list again and wait for another slot. In the meantime his eyesight began to deteriorate badly and he blames this on a lack of medication. Beneath dark sunshades, his eyes glimmer with hope, but he is not a happy man.

My advice, if Guido hadn't thought of it already was to sue the hospital. It was received as if I had hit an optical nerve, because he abruptly swivelled his bottom on the shiny granite surface to face me. He removed his tinted glasses and opened his eyelids wide, as if he was demonstrating to me his lack of vision and insisted I look into his eyes. I wondered why. Did he think I had the ability to restore sight? Then for some reason he wanted me to take an even closer look. A second later he asked me if I was looking into his eyes. I said I was (even though I wasn't) and he seemed to believe me. He then declared that he had been to see a lawyer about suing the hospital, but the lawyer had said there was no definitive proof that the lack of medication was the cause. Especially when the hospital insisted he was suffering from plain old age. But he continued to claim that their inefficiency was the cause, because he could see perfectly well before they neglected him.

It was chubby millionaire Mario's turn to join in the discourse. He'd obviously overheard the word "hospital" and it started him talking about his doctor's appointments, his high blood pressure, his unruly cholesterol, his intestinal pains and the severe stiffness in all his joints. He said he'd only left the doctors surgery ten minutes earlier and as if to prove it, he started to flick through a stack of prescriptions he was about to present to the pharmacy. Then, in case they hadn't already done so on previous occasions everyone wanted to tell me about their ever-present health issues. When they had more or less concluded, they informed me about what I must expect a few years down the line. I seem to get plenty of what I term "useless useful advice" from them on all matters under the sun. 'Never get old,' was their advice on this day. If you do, you'll be taking pills for everything; so many pills that when you walk you can hear yourself rattle. But worse, peeing and pooing will be unreliable and an erection will be a dim memory.'

'So what's the remedy for avoiding it?' I asked.

This question left them flummoxed, but as the union was about to break up for lunch (and it's imperative the wife's pasta is eaten al dente, or she'll leave it to ruin if they arrive a minute late), they all had to rush home. But before they did, they all agreed that the meaning of life was too big a subject to discuss at that moment and I'd have to wait for the resolution at some later date.

~~~

The next morning, the gang's almost interminable talk about illnesses and longevity gradually switches to the refuse collection strike in Naples and the chaos it was causing the unfortunate residents. They register their disgust at how millions of Italian taxpayers' euros has been spent in order to build enough incinerators to cope with the rubbish situation, but most of it has been syphoned off and tucked away by the Camorra, the Neapolitan Mafia. It is the oldest and the largest criminal organisation in Italy and, amongst other things it controls Naples' waste collection. Vittorio arrives late, with an early edition of *La Corriere della Sera* and the pink *La Gazzetta dello Sport* under his arm, specifically it seemed to talk about the football, but he is momentarily overruled by the majority who are still rattling on about the calamitous refuse collection service in Naples; how thousands of tons of stinking, seeping plastic bags are filling the streets instead of the incinerators, and how after ten months of deadlock the government has refused to throw any more money at it.

Their position is to let the Camorra collect it because they have been collecting government subsidies very efficiently but neglecting to do what it has been paid to do. The other shocking news of the day is the extraordinary high tumour rate amongst the Neapolitan residents who live near landfill sites. The newspaper headline reveals that for twenty years, Naples has been Europe's main dumping ground for illegal toxic waste, because the Camorra has been mixing it with the regular city waste. Heavy metals, industrial waste, chemicals and household garbage are frequently dumped on the roadside or burnt to avoid detection, which has led to severe soil and air pollution and major health problems.

According to Vittorio's newspaper, national strikes are in the offing. The government is insisting that they will need to raise the retirement age even further than they have done already, to sixty-five for women and sixty-seven for men and this news hasn't been accepted lightly by the workers. The row created by this has been gathering momentum throughout the country and nowhere more than in piazza Roma in Argegno. Why this should have been of such concern to the old boys is a curiosity, because they are already retired, but then they are a curious lot.

The next topic on the agenda is the latest hike in the price of *benzina* (petrol) and the exorbitant price of a *casa* (a house). But once again, why should these news topics raise the decibel level of the piazza, making all the passers-by turn round to see where it's coming from because they never travel outside the village and they'll never live anywhere else.

However, the most important subject of the daily news delivery is *il calcio* (the football) in *La Gazzetta dello Sport*. The poor form of the mighty three, AC Milan, Juventus and Inter Milan has been giving the *cognoscenti* around the fountain some concern for most of the season. Inter went out of the Champions League early on, whilst AC Milan is a pile of *merda* and Juventus are not much better. Sod the oil price, sod the house price, sod the problems the Neapolitans have with their rubbish and sod the government. The *Milanisti* are more concerned about why Berlusconi, their (then) prime minister and the owner of AC Milan is refusing his coach seventy million euro to buy Cristiano Ronaldo.

Mario, the ex-restaurateur, an ardent Juventus fan is having a bad time. His team has been found guilty of match fixing and severe penalties were inflicted upon them. The Juvé calamity left him disillusioned, so there was little in his day for him to be pleased about. His nights at home cannot be much better either, because five years ago his wife consigned him to a single bed in the spare room. At resent she is away, visiting her sister in Sydney for four months and he is clearly distraught, because without her he says there was nobody to cook his meals or look after him, and if he should fall ill, who would call the ambulance? His only comfort is his huge stash of money; it seems that if it weren't for that, he'd be uncertain she'd ever come back. Another worry that could force him into premature illness is what to do, before he dies with all the interest accumulating in his bank. I cannot resist winding him up, so I made a suggestion. 'With all your money, why don't you buy yourself a new body, a younger wife and your own football team?'

I'd bet he's reflected on it many times and he gives me a look as if I can read his mind. He frowns and looks down at the pavement as if he needs to refocus. He then lifts his head and looks at me again, the corners of his mouth pointing downwards. Maybe he is thinking it could work, but what, he said was, 'what would be the point of outliving all my friends?'

What I should have suggested is that he should buy a new life as well as a new body and a younger wife. At seventy-two he is three years short of the average life expectancy of a man living in the EU. He knows he'll soon be on borrowed time, so I have to be careful what I say. All he knows is what he has taught himself, and if he strayed away from the fountain he'd be lost. His world has become a heavy burden. His eyelids and eyebrows droop, together matching the downward curvature of his mouth. Maybe, despite the pain in his joints he would be less tortured if only he appreciated the sun whilst he's around. The man still has a hunger in his eye and he still has ambition. He still has the capacity to do, and he tries to react against his confinement, but eventually he will capitulate, because he is bound by the convention that an elderly person should retire.

The old boys know that an inactive existence can become a way of life in itself. They have seen and done it all before. There is little or no excitement to be had from anything any longer, hence they daydream. They already know the inevitability of their lifestyle but they don't possess the imagination to alter its course.

~~~

In 2008, during our third year as residents of Argegno spring turned to summer too quickly and it caught our plants off guard. However, it had no effect on the old boys, because every season is the same for them. They cannot make love to the weather, they cannot buy and sell it and they cannot bottle it, so what use is it if there is no gain to be had?

A strong, dry breeze had been drifting over for some days and it had blown a layer of fine sand over from the Middle East. If windows had been left ajar and most of them had been, because it had been so hot - a fine covering of golden dust had landed on everything, inside and outside. This had convinced the old boys that the world's climate is dying as fast as they are, and they say the expiry date cannot be far away. 'What the hell,' they agreed. 'None of us as individuals can do anything about anything. It's the sods that suck our blood who are to blame. It's the ones who back the economists and the oil tycoons who poison us with their fumes. Fortunately we'll all be gone by the time it really hits us.'

During the later war years, alongside their parents, the eldest of the old boys fought a visible enemy that enslaved them, starved them and raped their mothers and their sisters, but this enemy is more serious. It has no boundaries and no allies. It has the smell of corporate collusion and they are very uneasy about it.

8 Beside the Seaside

In the early 1980s, when we were living in England, we'd visit Italy, particularly to Venice, Florence and Rome, and I took the opportunity to study high quality artwork that decorated the large villas, civic buildings, churches and cathedrals and hopefully to learn from it. My speciality is Trompe l'Oeil, meaning literally to trump or to fool the eye and despite it being known by a French name, it is an Italian creation. The Italians originally called it *chiaroscuro*, which translates directly as "light and dark". This doesn't mean anything in itself, because that is the basic requirement of all forms of painting. When the technique spread across Europe, and later throughout the world, the French gave it the name Trompe l'Oeil, the trick of making the eye believe it is looking at something in three dimensions, when in fact it is looking at a two dimensional image. It is, in short the art of deception.

When we came to live in Italy, I imagined that, as a foreigner who couldn't speak a word of Italian my chances as an artist of finding any work would be difficult. There was so much high quality art in Italy, so I anticipated that I, a British artist attempting to offer the Italians what they already had, would be akin to the old English saying, "taking coals to Newcastle." However, I soon found out that there weren't many artists, or at least professional ones producing new works in the traditional style. It appeared to have died centuries earlier, along with the masters that created it. There were a lot of specialist restorers of both wall paintings and antique paintings on canvas, but I wasn't interested in restoration work, so there wasn't likely to be any conflict of interests. However, that didn't mean I was going to be inundated with calls for new work like I had been in England in the days when the economy had been good, and I soon found out that the well to do Italian, in the process of updating his interior decoration didn't necessarily want a mural or two. It turned out that there was precious little new mural work being added to the already overwhelming amount that is around. However, I must have made an impression on a Swedish friend of Elaine Masin when I showed her my portfolio, because she said her husband had a business colleague who was the leading architect in the Como area and she would tell him to organise a meeting for me with that architect. Over a period of some time, the Como architect turned out to be a sometimes good and a sometimes not so good provider of work. He was possibly better known in Italy as a playboy than as an architect, marrying a succession of famous women, a lifestyle that made him a regular face in the glossy magazines and a frequent name in the gossip columns.

Despite the advice of local tradesmen not to touch him with a bargepole, I gave the man a try. I worked for him on several projects, painting murals in the homes of some of Italy's wealthiest citizens, which helped take the strain off our bank account. At the beginning of our working relationship he was fine and I was glad to find the sort of work I'd been privileged to enjoy in the UK, but later he became scornful and began paying me what he felt like paying me, despite the price having already been agreed. It was like working for an agent who retains anything from ten to sixty per cent, and until the job was finished there was never any certainty as to what I would actually end up with in my pocket. He was the sort of person who hadn't got to the top of his tree by being nice to people and he had a reputation throughout the region not just as an architect and playboy but also as a complete swine. It wouldn't have been worth my while making a fuss about the financial injustice because he would have ignored it if I had, and on some of the commissions I painted for him I lost money, but I stuck with him because of his importance and the size of the projects he offered me.

I was surprised to discover that when he is employed by a client to create their multi-million-euro dream home they must have complete faith in him, because they give him carte blanche. After the design is agreed and he's had their home built and furnished, he equips it with everything they are going to need, right down to the coffee spoons on the dining table. The day the clients move into their new home it will contain a fabulous kitchen, plenty of fitted out en suite bedrooms, a Jacuzzi or two, a sauna, a heated outdoor swimming pool and maybe an indoor one as well. There will also be a long, tree-lined driveway with a row of double garages at the end of it, along with a guest annex and an instant, fully mature, walled garden.

It has to be said that the results look magnificent and would deserve congratulation, but I'm not always sure his clients do congratulate him, because although they are likely to be happy with what he has created for them, they will not be happy with the amount of money it will have cost. On most of the projects he involved me in, the initial estimate for the whole build had increased by twenty-five per cent by the time it was finished and his clients had been left, at least concerned if not dismayed. I've also been further surprised, when I've been in moments of conversation with the architect and he's told me things in confidence about his work ethic; things his clients would undoubtedly be concerned about if they had known about them before they had employed him.

He must have trusted that I would not repeat to any of his clients what he told me, and I never did, but he will only take on jobs for multi-millionaire clients who are in business and he will have checked them out first to see if they and their businesses are solvent. He also told me his basic fee starts at a straight million euros and if they quibble, he tells them to find somebody else. He also said that once the plans have been drawn-up, the client has given the go-ahead for the work to start and they've handed over a down payment, it is too late for them to pull out because if they do, he won't return the down-payment. He also told me that within a year or two of their dream home being finished, the client would have recouped the outlay through their business or businesses, so if they complain about the spiralling cost he turns a deaf ear. It took me a few projects to learn his system and on some of them, if he didn't think I'd charged enough in my estimate he would tell me to load the price, because the client could afford it!

At first, I naively thought that I was going to receive the additional money, but what I received (if I was lucky) was the figure I had quoted him in my original written price before he told me to load it. On several projects I did, he actually told me the price I had to charge the client, which would always be a lot more than I had intended. From then on, I would be paid an anticipo (a down payment) in cash or a cheque, signed by the client. I would keep that, but once my job was finished and I'd paid my final cheque into my bank, I had to withdraw an amount in cash to pass onto the architect. It was always the amount he'd told me to load onto my estimate. But this wasn't the end of it, because I still had to pay him his agent's percentage, which, as I said before, was always an unspecified amount. At first I thought it was only me he was taking from, but one day I met a tradesman who was a specialist in the plastering technique of *Stucco Veneziano* who happened to be in litigation with the architect over payment. It was he who told me that this was how the architect's system worked, and that went for everybody who worked for him.

I stuck with the architect for a while because I wasn't overloaded with work and he knew how much to sting me for but still leave me with enough so I wouldn't be too downhearted to be available the next time he needed my services. He had a large network of wealthy contacts that could keep me in work for as long as I wanted, if I kept my nose clean.

When we bought the villa in Argegno I had temporarily stopped working for him, because I had to spend a lot of time working on the place. I'd also been painting murals for my own clients. Then, one morning the phone rang. It was the architect, calling on his mobile, demanding an appointment in his Como office that afternoon. Because I hadn't been in contact with him for a while I had forgotten how lax his timekeeping was, so when he said a four o'clock appointment he really meant five. I arrived on time, as always, as people with good manners are supposed to do, but after about forty minutes, during which I'd paced around his silent waiting room and flicked through a couple of architectural magazines I'd still had no word from him, or any explanation as to why he was late. With some Italians, punctuality, or lack of it can be infuriating, but he was particularly exasperating and I never found out why that was. Maybe it was supposed to give the impression he was busy, or he was insinuating that the meeting he'd called wasn't important to him. Let's say that I found his concept of time to be more fluid than mine. Eventually he arrived, with a roll of plans under his arm. After spending half an hour going through them, I agreed to a two-month stint, based on the culture of honouring a word and no contract. We would be working in a palace that had just been bought by an *avvocato* (a lawyer) on the

Italian Riviera.

At ten minutes past nine the next morning I met the architect for a caffè and brioche at an Autogrill on the A9 motorway, halfway to Milan. As usual he was late, but only by twenty minutes. From there we did the rest of the journey to the Riviera in his Porsche 911 3.6-litre Twin Turbo. It was a 300-kilometre white-knuckle ride and we arrived in what must have been a record time for a car. At times, as we cornered, I was literally pinned by g-forces to the seat. It brought to mind the exhilarating rides I had spent on the Big Dipper at Blackpool's Pleasure Beach. I didn't know if I was supposed to be flattered when he told me he was once a professional rally driver for Alfa Romeo. As we got out of the Porsche I also remember thinking that was only half the journey completed. After dinner with the client, we still had the return trip to make, and in the dark.

The palace was set in the centre of the seaside town of Albenga, in Liguria. It dated from the 17th century and was built in the Austrian style with four floors, a vaulted ceiling and thick walls. When we arrived, the building contractor had finished the structural renovation and was in the process of removing the scaffolding from the outside of the building. The project had obviously been huge, because although the palace was an extremely solid structure, it had been in a poor state. The lawyer had bought it for his office premises and it had needed complete refurbishment, inside and out. Everything was new, including the roof, the internal and exterior doors, windows and shutters and a lift system had been installed. Next on the agenda was the interior decoration. The morning we arrived, the office shelving, the bookcases and the desks were being installed. The architect and the lawyer showed me around the palace, briefing me on what they wanted painting and in which rooms. Mainly, they wanted me to design and paint deep, elaborate borders around the top of the walls just below the ceilings in the principal room and then restore a twenty-metre square, three hundred year old painted ceiling in the lawyer's office.

It was a *subito* - a 'must do', an immediate project. As he opened successive sets of solid double doors to the rooms he wanted decorating, the architect kept pouring instructions into my ear. But what I discovered was that most of the walls had been newly plastered and they still hadn't been sealed, nor had the primer coats been applied, so a decorator had to apply the base coats before I could start. The avvocato's office on the first floor was the priority; and at twenty square metres, it was large. The entrance hall was also a priority, followed by the stairwell, which ran up three of the four floors, then the reception area, the boardroom, the waiting rooms and some of the lawyer's partners' rooms. The second part of the project was to include the lesser offices, where a host of secretaries were to work. I estimated there was about two months' worth of preparation work for an *imbianchino*, a painter and decorator before I would be able to start, so I told them to telephone me when he'd finished. However, that wasn't satisfactory to either the architect or to the client. They wanted me to work in tandem with an imbianchino, starting in five days' time on the following Monday morning. As soon as he had finished the preparation work on one wall, they insisted I paint the border at the top of it the moment the base coats were dry. So, before I'd even started there was a wrangling match because they wanted me to employ the imbianchino, but I refused to do so. I didn't want the responsibility of employing anyone, because I would have to pay him rather than the architect pay him. I was well aware that this architect tried his best to retain his clients' money for his own purposes, so I said I wasn't interested in doing the job unless he found an imbianchino and he paid him.

As it was, neither the architect nor the lawyer could find an imbianchino in Albenga who was available to start work on the Monday morning, so the architect looked towards Como to find one. There weren't any in Como interested in working three hundred kilometres away from home for an architect who had a reputation as a complete swine, so in the end, he had to employ an imbianchino from Bergamo. The imbianchino, I later discovered, didn't know about the architect's reputation and he'd been pleased to be offered such a large contract, but the architect wasn't so pleased because, as it was a "hurry up" job, the imbianchino had said he would need an assistant to help him and that meant it would cost him more in labour than the architect wanted to pay. There was further wrangling ahead because, like me the imbianchino and his assistant needed accommodation for two months and there was a problem about who was going to pay for it. Eventually, it was agreed that the lawyer would find and pay for an apartment for the three of us. The wrangling increased when I said I wanted my own apartment as I wasn't happy about staying in the same apartment for two months with people I'd never met or worked with before, but this was refused.

Three weeks later - not in the five days the client and the architect had hoped for - I met Raul, the imbianchino and his assistant, Antonio in the entrance hall of the palace and then we collected the key for the apartment from the letting agency. We could only have the place for a month. Albenga is a popular summer holiday destination, as are all the towns along the whole Italian Riviera and the apartment was already booked for the holiday season beyond that time, but we were told not to worry, because the agency said they would find us another one by then.

The apartment the lawyer had booked for us was on the fifth floor of a typical 1970s purpose built holiday condominium, in an estate of identical blocks. We didn't realise it was a holiday home at the time, because it was on the opposite side of the town from the sea, and as it was still early in the season only a few of the apartments were occupied. Our apartment was situated two kilometres from the town centre and apart from a pizzeria and a pharmacy there wasn't much in the way of amenities within walking distance. It had obviously been cheap to rent, because it was basic and tired, with no cleaning materials provided except for a hand broom with a worn out head and a cracked plastic dustpan. There were a few cooking utensils, but they were well worn and greasy. I presumed that the families who rent the apartments must fill their car with everything they need for self-catering before they set off, otherwise it would be a case of spending a small fortune paying out for the basics. On the plus side, there was a large fridge and the water system worked well. There were two double bedrooms, and although the bedding supplied was inadequate, it didn't matter because it was so hot that we would only need sheets. The decorators and I were a bit nonplussed as to what we were going to do about the sleeping arrangements, but they quickly decided to share a double bed, thankfully leaving me with the other double room. To assure me they weren't gay, they both told me they were married with children. Antonio had only married a couple of months before, but his child was four. Nicola and I weren't married at the time, but I told them about her, and that she would vouch that I was very much heterosexual. The sleeping arrangements were only temporary; Raul snored so loudly that Antonio moved on to the divan in the lounge for the duration. As it was, he only had to withstand the discomfort for four nights each week, because as soon as we had finished on a Friday evening we left for our homes. The return trip on Monday mornings wasn't so accommodating, because it meant they had to leave Bergamo at 4.30am, and I half an hour earlier in order to arrive in Albenga together.

We started work on the palace in the middle of the June, and it was flaming hot. The palace was only two hundred metres from the Gulf of Italy and the beach was beginning to fill up with bodies as the temperature rose even higher. We knew that by August, when the whole country closes down for the annual holiday, the beach would be bursting.

After we had settled into the apartment, we went to find the town's paint store to buy the acrylic sealant and the emulsion paint the imbianchini would need for the preparation work, along with the artist's paints I would need. There was a lot of it - the total cost came to €2000. We then took it to the palace, where I would be mixing the base colours for the decorators. It was a painstaking as well as long job: because each room had a different colour scheme, therefore, they needed a different base colours. Also the ceilings of the palace were vaulted and I wanted to spray them with dark tones at the sides, graduating to white at the top of the vault, so we had to hire a large compressor and spray guns.

After our first day's work we went to a bar opposite a supermarket in the centre of town and sat outside with a cold beer each to discuss what we were going to do about our domestic arrangements. If anybody had been listening in, especially Nicola, they would undoubtedly have found our discussion amusing. How often do three middle-aged men, who had never met before that day, sit down to talk about organising their domestic chores? Fortunately we discovered that we all liked the same foods, so that was a good start. We also agreed that we weren't going to be able to eat out every night, because although we had asked for a subsistence allowance, it hadn't been provided. The client, like the architect, didn't get rich by being considerate to the likes of us. Food can be expensive, so we knew we would have to plan our limited budget carefully over the following weeks. Either we could eat pizza every night, which was fairly cheap but monotonous, or we could cook our own food. So, while we were sitting outside the supermarket I suggested to Raul and Antonio that we should go on our second buying trip of the day and stack up with food and cleaning materials to take back to the apartment, but they seemed a bit hesitant about taking charge of a shopping trolley. They understood why we would have to eat in, but they hesitated about going shopping, because they were Italian men. They had never had to cook anything before in their lives, because their wives always did it for them and their mothers had done it for them before that therefore, food shopping wasn't in their upbringing either. Nevertheless, I took charge, pushing the trolley along the aisles with the other two hanging back like a couple of mules on a rope. More astoundingly, it was the first time in their working lives they had worked away from home. This is typical for an Italian tradesman, who will rarely take on a job that is more than a twenty-minute drive from his home, otherwise it would mean forfeiting lunch. It became clear I was going to have to train Raul and Antonio in what was unnatural to them; how to decide what they were going to eat, where to find it and how to live without a female to look after them.

Back at the apartment, after we had unloaded the shopping we opened a bottle of Morellino, tipped some green olives into a bowl, loaded a plate each with slices of pecorino cheese and anchovies on crackers and moved outside to sit on our tiny balcony to continue the discussion about domesticity. We'd bought enough food and drink for a couple of nights, but we needed to plan some menus for the rest of the week. They seemed only too willing, and I believe relieved, to allow me to take charge, so I suggested leaving the food and cooking up to me. I' knew I wouldn't have much energy left after a hard day's work in summer heat, so for me to start cooking in the evening was no mean undertaking. Nevertheless, we struck a deal where I would cook if they agreed to do the supermarket shopping according to my list while I sat in an air-conditioned bar across the street with a beer, then they would wash up and clean the apartment.

One of the dishes I cooked for them was *spaghetti aglio olio e peperoncino* (spaghetti with extra virgin olive oil flavoured with fresh garlic, and fresh, red chilli peppers). The first time I ate it was in a trattoria in Moltrasio and it became one of those dishes I had to learn how to cook and add to my repertoire. It only has only four ingredients, but they come together to make a display of fireworks in the mouth that most people never forget. The two imbianchini, who were native *Bergamasci* (from Bergamo) liked it as much as I did, which is unusual, because northern Italians don't normally go for *piccante* (spicy) food, or at least not as spicy as I, or southern Italians like it. I've tried spaghetti aglio olio e peperoncino in several trattorie in different parts of Italy since the one in Moltrasio, and even Nicola agrees that they don't compare to my version. I don't know what it is about chilli dishes, but I think the ingredient is addictive, which is maybe why Indian food is so popular in the UK. Raul and Antonio said that my spaghetti aglio olio e peperoncino was the best they'd ever tasted. Asking them what they wanted for dinner became a standing joke, because every time I did they would say 'the same as last night!' I get great satisfaction from cooking Italian food for Italians better than they can cook it. It is the same for Nicola when she does her polenta: it will be the best they'll ever taste in Italy.

Lunch was the next item for consideration. This also proved a problem during our first few days, because all we found near the palace were trendy bars that served salad-filled panini: expensive at between €6 and €10. Raul in particular wasn't content with a single panino for lunch, so he asked a group of builders we came across where they ate. They pointed us in the direction of a Chinese restaurant that wasn't too far from the palace, which provided a *pranzo di lavoro* (workman's lunch) for a special price of €12 per head. The restaurant cooked Italian food as well as Chinese, so during our second week we decided to give it a try. Antonio and I quite liked the three-course meal we had and I thought it good value, but it was a Chinese version of Italian cooking. Raul wasn't keen on it, because it wasn't the same as the real thing and the portions weren't big enough for him, so he wanted to find somewhere else that did a proper pranzo di lavoro.

The second month arrived and we had to move to another apartment. We had been hoping that the agents might have found us a better place to stay, but they gave us a flat in an identical condominium down the road. The only difference was that we were on the third floor rather than the fifth, but like the first place, nothing worked efficiently, but we coped. Then Raul found a trattoria that did the traditional pranzo di lavoro. It was a twelve-kilometre round trip every day, but it was worth it, because the food was good and the portions were large enough to keep us going, and for €11 a head, including half a litre of wine each. It worked out well, because we could eat something lighter in the evenings, which meant less cooking, less food shopping and much less washing up. This was a welcome relief for all of us.

The intense heat had arrived early that summer and to make matters worse, the humidity levels were high. I'd been hoping that the weather on the coast would be fresher than inland, but there was precious little difference. The Italians don't use air conditioning units very much. August is hot enough for air-conditioning, but few people install it because the country closes down for a month and everyone goes to the coast to cool down in the sea. However, August and national holiday time was still some weeks away and we had no alternative but to work through the heat. There was no escaping it, even with all the palaces windows wide open, because there was no wind. Ceiling fans would have been welcome, but the electrical fittings weren't yet installed, so we just had to sweat it out. As an artist, all I usually need is an apron to protect my clothes, but as there was a lot of spray painting to be done, I wore one piece industrial overalls with nothing on underneath except a pair of underpants, plus a hat, as did Raul and Antonio. Even this wasn't ideal, because the overalls became clammy with sweat.

The nature of the job varied according to whatever part of the building we were working on. On some days it was a case of scrambling up and down dusty scaffolding towers, pulling up buckets of paint on the end of a rope, and on others we were hanging over a twenty-five metre high stairwell. At the end of the day I looked more like a chimney sweep than an artist. Perspiration poured off us and made for a thoroughly unpleasant first few weeks' work, especially in the afternoons, when temperatures reached thirty-nine degrees and humidity levels rose to the nineties. Still, one good thing to come out of the heat was that the paint dried more or less as it was applied, so we could apply the second coats straight away. After the imbianchini had finished preparing one wall I would draw the designs across the top of the walls from the designs I had done and the imbianchini would fill them in with specified colours. Because hot air rises, painting at the top of the wall was like working in a sauna. We drank bottled water in huge quantities and we prayed for lunchtime, because it was a chance to put the air conditioning on in Raul's van on the journey to the trattoria. In the evenings, as soon as six o'clock arrived, we ran down the road, crossed the beach, removed our sticky overalls and, leaving them where they fell waded out into the sea until the deeper water felt colder than the air temperature around us. After our dip in the sea, an air-conditioned bar was the next port of call, and there was one on the road to the apartment. After that we returned to the apartment to eat and then get ready to go out for the evening.

Since arriving in Italy I'd always worked alone, because the commissions I'd been given had been comparatively small. Working and cohabiting alongside two others wasn't something I'd planned on. Now, Raul, Antonio and I were spending all our waking and sleeping hours in each other's company. I was seeing more of them during the week than I did of Nicola, so understanding each other became paramount. It got to the point where we did everything together, including socialising, not only because we didn't know anybody else in the area but also because we liked each other's company.

Before this, I'd never lived with Italians who had to work for a living, so when I took on the job the architect had offered me, I had not, for one second considered living arrangements being important. However, when I was obliged to share accommodation with two complete strangers it became necessary to do so. I discovered that their way of going about their ablutions and personal preparations were somewhat different from mine. Suddenly, the little domestic details I took for granted became significant and the new arrangements took some getting used to. The morning routine was all rush. First thing in the morning the coffee pot went on the gas stove and there would be a brief battle for the bathroom. They didn't shower, and I'm not sure they cleaned their teeth. By the time they'd splashed their faces and dressed, the coffee would be percolating. They'd take a straight caffè espresso, almost too hot to drink, half stirred with no milk, a lot of sugar and a cigarette and they'd be starting up the van ready to leave within fifteen minutes of rising. To their disgust my early morning procedure was different from theirs and it drove them crazy. I would have tea rather than coffee, then I would have a shower and a shave, clean my teeth and get dressed. This would take me at least half an hour, but while I was hurrying as much as I could, they would be cooling their heels in the van and smoking more cigarettes. After the first week they got fed up with having to wait for me and they would inevitably telephone my mobile while I was still in the bathroom, telling me they needed to go and I would have to follow in my car. However, when I did as they said and arrived at the palace to start work they were never there. So what was the rush for if it wasn't work? No, their priority was the bar across the road from the palace where they had their second fix of the day before starting work. This consisted of a vital fourth cigarette each and another espresso with a large shot of Sambuca in it, a cream filled brioche, another cigarette and sometimes a glass of red wine.

Every evening after work, while I sipped cold beer on the tiny balcony, Raul and Antonio engaged in a ritual fight over who was going to use the bathroom first. Raul was around forty years old and Antonio was in his early thirties, so Raul would usually claim superiority by virtue of age. If Antonio didn't accept that, Raul told Antonio that as he was his boss he had better respect him or he would sack him. And if even that didn't work, Raul would strong-arm his way through the door. It was understandable to some extent why there was a battle, because once Raul was in the bathroom he was in there for a long time. After a good soak in the bath, with salts, he would powder himself, clean his teeth, shave, splash cologne all over himself and then blow-dry and gel his hair. Antonio took exactly the same amount of time as his boss and probably did the same things in the same order, although he argued that he didn't take as long. Raul would dress in a white, short-sleeved shirt and lightweight grey trousers and slip on shoes without socks. Antonio chose fashion jeans and a red, green or blue sweatshirt. While they were preparing themselves for the evening, I got dinner ready. After dinner they would wash the dishes and tidy the kitchen while I used the bathroom. I didn't shave, because I did that in the morning and I didn't blow dry my hair or apply powder or overbearing aftershave, because I never do. I was ready in a quarter of the time they took and then, always before I was ready, they'd be anxious to be off out. Generally we went to town in my car, because it looked cooler than driving around in Raul's van. We'd park in the same side street and more often than not in the same space we used in the mornings, which was not that far from the palace. Then we would start our *passeggiata*, the Italian ritual evening walk.

The roads in the towns along the Ligurian coast are laid out in a grid formation, and those closer to the beach are divided into a series of lanes that run for hundreds of metres parallel to the coast. These lanes are a famous feature and they are full of brightly lit shops, bars, trattorie and restaurants that stay open late into the evening. The towns buzz with tourists buying clothes, souvenirs and food or sitting outside a bar or under the awnings of a trattoria or restaurant, drinking, eating and smoking. There was also a promenade, where there are more bars. And there is the sea, for a late night swim. Most Italians use the beach in the daytime when they can get the required suntan, so in the evenings the beaches are likely to be deserted, because if they swam in the evening they would have to forsake the *bella figura* (the beautiful look) as the talcum powder, the hair gel, the cologne and the rest of it get washed away in the sea. I thought it a waste of the climate, because the British rarely have the luxury of warm seawater at night.

You cannot have everything in life, but Raul and Antonio thought they could, and they weren't getting dressed up for nothing. It seemed inappropriate, even odd that we three were strolling around with the holidaymakers in one of the most famous parts of Italy when we weren't on holiday. And although we tried to look as if we fitted in, we felt like imposters. Where everyone else was letting their hair down, we knew we had to be up by seven-thirty prompt, so we had to act responsibly. I was content to take the cooler evening air, not missing the sweat pouring off my body all day, just watching people enjoying their holiday from a seat outside a bar but that wasn't enough for Raul and Antonio and before too long, my memories of working with Claudio, my fat, black-bearded "artist" friend returned. They, like Claudio, were working miles away from their homes and their spouses, and it was happening for the first time in their lives. They were in an area that was beginning to hum with single women from the fashion set and they couldn't wait to get stuck into them.

They chose a particular karaoke bar as their main port of call. However, the main attraction wasn't watching and listening to people making fools of themselves. Raul was certain the barmaid and her mother were in love with him, so we had to spend a small fortune in their bar so he could take whatever opportunity he could to lay on the chat. Very soon I'd had enough of this; the work at the palace was gruelling and I was too exhausted to stay out late like them, chatting up women so I started to stay in and go to bed early. They resented this and they accused me of being old before my time, so I did let them browbeat me into going out once a week and then in separate vehicles so that I could drive back when I wanted to.

They accepted this, but then, one night they conned me.

It was a Wednesday night, when they said they had found another music venue and I imagined it was another karaoke bar. That was what they let me believe, but when we got there it turned out to be a "night." They hadn't had any luck in the streets or in the bars finding available women, so a house of ill repute had become their last resort.

Monitoring the activities of a brothel, especially an Italian one was not something I had ever imagined doing, because it is one of many things in this life I never had any interest in, but for the second time within two years, it's what I found myself doing. The economy may have been in recession, but there didn't appear to be a downturn in the sex industry. Business was booming. On Nicola and my visit to Nardo's "night" in Switzerland, I counted fifteen prostitutes on duty there, and in our hour and a half there, around thirty-five men engaged with them, but with this one in Albenga there were thirty girls dealing with more than seventy clients within the same time span. When a client arrived, a hostess would escort him to the bar and when he'd had a drink he would be shown to a table, where he would watch two naked pole dancers doing their stuff to piped pop music. Then, after another drink or two, some prostitutes would approach him. He would select one, who would then take him up a sweeping, curved staircase to an individual room above. Who the clients were and where they came from was also interesting, because they looked like an eclectic mix of Arabs and Orientals, with a few Europeans who, apart from our two from Bergamo didn't seem to be Italian. The common language was Italian, even though none of the prostitutes were Italian. They all appeared to be familiar with their clients and vice versa, which strongly suggested that the clients were regulars. Raul and Antonio visited the brothel twice more, but I didn't accompany them and then at the end of July, we, along with the rest of Italy finished work for the summer holiday.

Six weeks later we reunited in yet another apartment, in yet another housing block. I'd worked at home during August, painting a piece of Trompe l'Oeil furniture for an American client. Raul and Antonio, having holidayed together in Sardinia with their families, came back tanned and bearing presents. Their van was loaded with Sardinian salami, spicy pickled tinned sardines, blood sausages with mint and thyme, *formaggio pecorino* (ewe's cheese) and bottles of Sardinian vino rosso, bought from the vineyard for fewer euros per bottle than we'd pay for water. Before going to bed that night we had a party.

They tried their best to continue their holiday spirit for as long as they could, but the season was coming to an end. The holiday homes were emptying and the few that remained occupied contained the elderly. Working in a holiday resort out of season is tedious. The last of the long limbed, olive skinned beauties were rolling-up their beach towels and heading back home. All Raul and Antonio could do was dwell on their memories and lost opportunities. In the evenings, the once bright lights in the shops seemed dimmer, the bars were three-quarters empty and the bustle of the season had gone. When I asked Raul and Antonio if they were going to the karaoke bar or the vibrant 'night', they said they couldn't afford them any longer. I didn't imagine for a second they'd had a character change and I was waiting to see how they would react once they received their next pay cheque, but when they did, they seemed to be content, like I was, to sit on our little balcony indulging in an antipasto of tinned sardines and sipping Sardinian wine, or watching TV. Their only substitute for the hot sex they used to look forward to was eating my spaghetti aglio olio e peperoncino every night.

~~~

Once a week the architect would drive all the way from Como to see how we were getting on with "his" schedule and inevitably to "kick ass". Even though we were always doing well, he would still kick ass. The client would do the rounds with him and because he was artistically ignorant, he didn't understand what we were doing and he would repeat, parrot-fashion the architect's comments. Because all Italian palaces are lavishly decorated with art work, all the client knew was that his palace needed decoration too, so to try and give us and the architect the impression he did know what he was talking about, he thought he would add his penny's worth of "ass-kicking" as well.

Both the architect and the client applied pressure over the telephone as well as in person, impressing on us that the job was urgent because the lawyer wanted to move himself and his staff into his palace "yesterday". It was an old story the two imbianchini and I have heard many times before, because as decorators we are always the last contractors on site. The builders will have finished and gone, or they will be working outside and the rest of the tradesmen will be packing up and leaving as I am just beginning, and generally the deadline for the building to be handed over to the client will have passed weeks before I start. By the time I arrive, the client will probably have been waiting for months, if not years to move into his new home. His tolerance level will be low and he will feel he cannot wait any longer. In consequence he will try and drive me to paint as fast as I can move a paintbrush, but all I ever promise is that I will work as fast as I can. This will never be good enough and within minutes of my saying so, he will apply the pressure once again, as if he hadn't heard what I said. It was the same scenario in the UK when architects and their clients wanted their projects finished within a couple of days of my arriving on site, in an attempt to make up for the shortfall in time, when they were well aware I was scheduled to be there for weeks.

In the case of this avvocato, he had just bought himself a large villa in the mountains overlooking Albenga that, like the palace needed complete refurbishment and artwork, so the reason he gave us for giving us the hurry up was that the sooner we had finished his palace, the sooner we could start on his new home, because his family were staying in rented accommodation and they needed to move out of it.

One blissful September evening, after we had finished the day's work, the imbianchini and I decided we would take a drive to the client's villa in the mountains to look at the next project he'd said was ready for us to start on. It was a two-hundred-year old, five-bedroom villa, surrounded by trees and mountains and with a view over the Gulf of Italy as far as Monte Carlo. When we introduced ourselves to the *capo di cantiere* (the builders' foreman) he was closing up the site for the evening, but when we told him it was likely we would be doing the decoration, he let us have a quick glance at the inside of the building. The whole place was gutted, and the foreman told us that his company had been working on the villa for five months, mainly on demolition work and reinforcing the foundations, the drains and the access road, and there would be at least another eight months' work reinstating the walls, the ceilings and the staircase, as well as building a new guest annex that we had also been asked to decorate, before we could be called in to start. In other words, like the palace, it was a total refurbishment job that was nowhere near ready for us to begin, despite the avvocato telling us it was.

I had to give the client credit for his tenacity, because he came around every evening after he'd finished his work to see what we had been doing, and of course to push us along. The imbianchini and I had to remain patient, while at the same time reassuring him that the decoration was on schedule, because that was what he wanted to hear. In the end, the project took three months to finish and not the two the architect had said it would take, not because of any failing on our part but because the client kept adding more rooms to paint. As he did so, he kept going on about how much we were costing him. He should worry, with two Ferraris in the garage, a Range Rover Freelander for a run-about and a Mercedes convertible for his wife, a palace for an office, a five-bedroom villa in the mountains and a trip to London with the architect, staying at Claridge's, where their intention was to buy an antique inlaid mahogany dining table and twelve chairs for the palace boardroom, costing £80,000.

When the lawyer's villa was ready for painting, I thanked the architect and the client for asking me to do it, but privately I meant "maybe". Raul and Antonio also wanted me to do the job with them, but I didn't want the hassle. The recession was biting and they needed the work. In the end I agreed to do an art project in the guest annexe, which took me three weeks to finish, but that was the last project I ever did for the Como architect. I'd decided that it was time for him to kick someone else's ass for a change. I didn't need him any more, because I had made other plans.

9 Povera Italia

The following morning, when I arrived to take my seat at the fountain, the old boys were examining the sky, unsure whether they should stay where they were or retreat to the Bar Onda, in case the weather should change. The autumn equinox was due and the weather forecast didn't look promising. In the end they decide to sit it out to see if the heavens lightened or if bad light would stop play.

It is the end of 2012, and again an Italian general election is in the offing. It seems to be an annual ritual, as on-going as the seasons. To have sixty-one governments since the end of The Second World War is quite an achievement. As the reality of the economic situation bites into their personal finances it has triggered a stream of disgruntled comments from the regulars around the granite fountain. The combined stubbornness of the labour unions is breaking the country, they say. Intransigence, doggedness and out-of-date perceptions are crippling the unions' thinking, because they want an all-out strike. The old boys are united in wishing they had a Prime Minister with balls, who will change things. They look to me to provide another Margaret Thatcher, but I tell them that if someone like her took charge in Italy, she'd be assassinated in her first week.

"Basta" in Italian means "enough" and they've had it up to the neck with multi-phase inflation, the unyielding structure of the hierarchy and the credit crunch. Strict austerity measures are firmly in place and they seem to be getting more severe by the week. The euro is weak one week, the dollar strong the following week. Italy's principal industry is tourism, but where are the tourists this year? The old boys feel let down by the European Union since they voted "si" to the euro. They all know Italy cannot look after herself and they'd been led to believe all her problems would be put to bed with her succession to the big nanny European Union, but it seems the problems have only just started. In return for Italy joining the monetary union, Brussels thanked them for joining and welcomed them aboard, but now, as Italy desperately needs help to keep her economy afloat, Brussels sends a message back telling her to sort her own ship out.

The old boys are really hopping mad today, and their credence of the stories the newspapers print is minimal. Silvio Berlusconi was made to resign in 2011 after years of transgressions. Mario Monti was appointed as a technocratic Prime Minister. He says he doesn't want to stand in the forthcoming election because he feels he's banging his head against a brick wall. The official reason he gave was that he has lost the confidence of parliament, but there is talk he will form his own Monti party at the last minute. Septuagenarian Berlusconi has found himself in court several times in recent years. In October 2012 he was given a four-year prison sentence after being found guilty of tax fraud relating to TV rights bought by one of his companies, Mediaset, but it was reduced to a single year because of his political status. The three-times prime minister was also banned from holding public office for five years. Both penalties were suspended pending an appeal.

At another trial he received a year's sentence for wire tapping, which he is also appealing. Both appeals will take months to accomplish, but in the mean time he's announced he's going to have his sixth stab at being the country's leader, having said two months earlier that he was going to withdraw from politics. Now his slogan is, 'my people need me.' But do they? The reality is, Italy's domestic problems are varied and run so deep that whoever gets in will most likely be rendered ineffectual, because they always have been. The old boys are united in their negativity and end the morning session with a great big yawn.

Even the tourists stepping off the ferry are beginning to sense the unease Italy is feeling. Now that times are tough, Italy has stopped smiling. In years gone by, foreign tourists thought Italia was a soft touch, but now they don't like the place as much as they did. For decades, the country was easy going, with a bubbly personality. The traveller would pay anything for the pleasure of joining in with local culture, but not any longer. It is twelve years since the euro replaced the lira, but the pain is still being felt. Now that Italians are feeling-the-pinch they have suddenly become serious. Budget holidays are useless to Italy, because they don't show a profit.

The country is all but bankrupt, but as yet its people are not. The country is in recession, then it's out, then it's back in again. As I write this, it is hovering on the edge; with growth forecasts in the minus, so it's likely that it will be back in recession again very soon. The country has struggled for decades - perhaps that should be centuries - while its politicians and its people have defrauded each other. An aversion to paying their dues was common and it made everybody happy. However, by increasing tax contributions the interim Monti government has put the smile on the other side of people's faces. Now that pay back time has arrived, its people have changed character.

And that's another reason why the smiling Italian is a thing of the past.

Italians are Europe's most serious savers, and their first investment is likely to be a house or an apartment. Treasury bonds account for forty per cent of personal investments and the stock market is viewed with suspicion. Wealth fascinates Italians. The tabloids are full of articles describing the lifestyles of super-rich industrialists and film stars. The country's post-war economic prosperity happened within living memory but still there is an ever-present fear of a return to poverty. The thought of wearing shabby clothes, having to cut down on eating or running the same car for more than three years will bring a look of horror to most Italian faces.

The next morning the news from the daily rag is again received with gloom by the old boys, because the price of a barrel of crude has shot up again. Bruno is worried he will have to put his scooter in store if it continues to spiral. The chat turns to gas-guzzling cars and the possible end of Sunday motoring. I am the only one to applaud this statement and they scowl at me as if they think I've gone mad. For the Italian, the thought of life without a vehicle is absolutely inconceivable, although the thought of the country without a government is not only conceivable but for so much of their post-war history it has been a reality.

Christmas 2012 came and went without many people being interested in it and it was the same at New Year. The festivities were cloaked in despondency and darkness. A lot of the towns and cities played the season down by not putting up any fairy lights and in some of the villages, people pretended it wasn't happening. For the sake of the very young, parents made believe everything was normal, but for the kids over six-years-old it was obvious that it wasn't. Personally I'd never heard it so quiet and it was all because Monday the 25th of February 2013 was election day and it was going to be bigger than any Christmas celebrations. The day had overshadowed everything else for months because the country was in dire need.

There's an Italian saying, 'in most countries the political situation is serious but not desperate. In Italy it is desperate but not serious.' I cannot vote in an Italian general election because although I am a resident, I am not an Italian citizen. It may have been the final election in which some of the old boys would vote and I believe some of them were hoping it would be. The election was forecast to be tight, because over the weeks leading up to the moment, the opinion polls failed to identify a clear leader and nobody believed there would be one when the results were counted. The anticipation of voting is as thrilling as having teeth pulled, but people have to vote to try to save the country from ruin.

Then, a few months before the general election a television comedian, Bepe Grillo threw his hat into the political ring. Though popular in Italy, the rest of the world has never heard of him. Grillo's satirical gags made La Borsa (the Italian stock exchange) very jittery, and had unnerved the establishment. He first hit the scene in 2009 when he started to ridicule the mainstream parties, first on his TV show and later in his blog. He captivated viewers by hurling accusations of corruption and insults at the government and they hit a nerve. Many of the individuals he attacked couldn't do anything to defend themselves, because through the vehicle of comedy, Grillo told the truth. His victims were basically stuffed, and from those programmes he gathered a following of millions who began to believe he could change the situation for the better.

Grillo is well known amongst the old boys of Argegno, but on the whole they regard him as a fly-by-night (albeit a comical one), who wouldn't last five minutes in politics. It appeared that none of them took him seriously, so I asked them why, because a lot of what he said made sense. They did agree with a lot of what he said, but they maintained that he exaggerated so as to get laughs on TV, and anybody who took him as a serious political contender must be an oddball. On prodding them further it seemed that they thought, in this age where the politics of one country is examined by all the others, having Grillo representing Italy could make foreigners believe that all Italians are as out of the ordinary as he is: they believed Berlusconi's colourful reputation abroad was already something to be concerned about, so for him to be followed into the political arena by a comedian would be too much. Soon my questions ceased to be appreciated.

It snowed heavily on election weekend, making the turnout low, but when the results came in, no single group won a working majority. This was largely because of a huge protest vote, and Italy had a hung parliament once again! But the big upset was that one in four Italians, mostly students, the unemployed and housewives, who were neither left nor right and who had nothing in their pockets except anger and a lack of faith, voted for Bepe Grillo. Nobody in Italy imagined that Grillo's anti-establishment Cinque Stella (Five Star) Movement would capture this many votes, but they had, and his stunning election success propelled one-hundred and sixty-three of his supporters, known as *Grillini*, who consisted of students, housewives, nurses, teachers, jobless factory workers, graphic designers, engineers, bank clerks, biologists, architects, lawyers and an astrophysicist into the two houses of parliament. Five Star now had the whip hand. This was unprecedented for a newcomer in European politics, and it came as a shock to a lot of people who had underestimated this party of fresh-faced idealists with no experience of public life. Many of these newly elected senators and deputies had just passed the minimum age limit of twenty-five to stand for election. Almost as extraordinary was the fact that five days after the election results had been counted, some of the newly elected members met for the first time in a hotel room to thrash out a party line. 'Don't call us honourable members of parliament,' they said.' 'Call us citizens of the Republic.'

Grillo's message had been simple; Italian politics are corrupt, elitist and closed. The left and right have been in power for twenty-five years and all they have done is lead the country into catastrophe. Italy's problem is these people and they won't last much longer!

What had been a busy week for Italy got busier. Three days after the election, Pope Benedict XVI resigned. He said he hadn't got the energy to carry on, but the opinion amongst the disbelievers was that he was getting out whilst he had some credibility left. For centuries The Vatican had maintained its power and managed to keep improprieties under wraps, but rumours were rampant about corruption, money laundering and tax evasion within their own bank, as well as sexual misconduct. There were also rumours of ties with the mafia. The spectre of shame and disgrace was not likely to go away, so the feeling was that he was leaving it for somebody else to sort out.

This news seemed to be accepted, almost ignored by the Argegnini and I was intrigued as to why this was. I attended a Roman Catholic school as a child, but because it was a very short distance from my home this was possibly more out of convenience than religious association. Nevertheless, I was rigorously indoctrinated into the idea that the Roman Catholic Church could do no wrong. Any suggestion to the contrary was regarded with horror. Before I moved to Italy I was sure that all Italians were devout Catholics. I was expecting to live in a society where the Catholic faith was revered, but I was mistaken, because it has been no different from living in protestant England. In fact, I soon discovered there are a large proportion of Italians, particularly in the north, who are anti-Catholic out of principle, even though they were raised as Catholics from birth. The old boys were uninterested in the dark news coming from the Vatican, because it wasn't news to them. They had heard and digested the stories the world press were suddenly wallowing in decades ago. Their rather sneering view of the papal empire was to ask why it had only come to light now.

After the general election there were a couple more days of concern, as people discovered that not only was the Vatican rudderless but so was the country. There was little or no chance of agreement between the main parties to form a government. Grillo had won his votes by promising anti-austerity measures. He wanted an on-line referendum to pull Italy out of the Euro Zone, deep tax cuts in personal income, huge cuts in defence spending, huge increases in health spending, investment in the green economy, the cancellation of Italy's two trillion euro national debt, buying back six hundred billion euro of Italian bonds held by foreigners and then withdraw the country from the EMU. He also suggested that octogenarian Dario Fo, the Nobel Prize-winning playwright and satirist should be the next president. The old boys agreed with each other that Grillo was correct when he said that the establishment as it was wouldn't survive for much longer and the country needed a change.

It may well be coming, because those who were young adults in the war years are almost all gone; even the ones who were children at the time are slowly fading. After the war, they were the ones that kept traditions alive. They stayed in the family home and because it was full of memories they hung on to it like a security blanket. They respected continuity, but times have changed, and the youth say that now that the war generations have finally faded it's their turn to run things their way. Grillo did so well in the general election because it was mainly the computer-savvy young voters who voted for him. But now it's their turn, they find they are unemployed and the country is on its uppers, so whatever they have in mind to turn things around, they are tied by what the outside world will allow them to do. Few of the world's economies are performing well and there is little chance of growth. This eliminates opportunities for the young and so they are likely to leave Italy. There is little difference between the restrictions imposed upon the older generation and those imposed on the young.

Another week passed as Italians became even more disillusioned with the negative outcome of a general election they had been led to believe was going to get Italy on track, including a seriously anxious European Union, because they didn't have a figurehead with whom they could consult. Then another week went by as the main parties continued to negotiate a working majority. After another couple of weeks of wrangling, the only news still filling the TV screen was about the political deadlock. Finally and in some desperation, 88 year-old President Giorgio Napolitano invited Enrico Letta, the leader of the centre left Democratic Party to end the stalemate and form a grand coalition. Now, Letta was about to form the first government in the history of the Republic to include representatives of all the major candidate coalitions that had competed in the election.

Alas, as time proved this wasn't the answer. Within a matter of months, the centre left party were criticising Letta for not making any significant moves that Italy desperately needed and he began to receive some heavy pressure, mainly from the young mayor of Florence, the up and coming Matteo Renzi. He, like the public found that once again Italy was dragging its feet and that she needed urgency and vibrant, younger blood to affect decision-making. He declared that Italy, as the Eurozone's third-largest economy urgently needed a new, radical programme of badly needed reforms, and they needed to be pushed through.

News of these events was received around the fountain with typical cynicism.

'Thank God I'll be dead soon,' Pino says.
'The world is going mad.' Mario adds.
'The world is already mad,' another suggests.

It's been one of those times when the old boys are enjoying themselves by slagging everything off. The prerequisite seems to be who can gripe the most. They all want to join in and take a swipe, at everything and everybody. They bombard, complain, argue and browbeat, but nothing will be resolved. They are full of words but they offer no resolutions. They carp, they criticise and then they beg for help. They even beg me, and I try to offer them a different point of view. I suggest that perhaps Italy would function better without a government. It seems to me it has often been the creator of many problems, like excessive personal taxation or unnecessary and overpriced work projects, so without a majority to form a government, it is less likely our private bank accounts will be raided to make up the shortfall. But when I speak, none of them listen. Their frustrations have already been aired, so I tell them they have no cause to complain about anything because they have everything they need. I tell them they are the lucky ones, who by accident of birth live in a beautiful location and they have nine of hours' sunshine a day, but all they talk about is what they haven't got.

'What does he know?' they chorus.

At the end of the morning session, as if to summarise the entirety of their lifetimes spent pontificating, their common grievance is reduced from the nation's political standing to the insufficient number of women they have made love to.

As it turned out, after a lot of behind the scenes political in-fighting Matteo Renzi, nicknamed "Il Rottamatore" (the scrapper) who had built up a substantial fan base by rejecting so-called "old politics" and its backroom deals, engineered the removal of the sitting Prime Minister Letta by calling a vote for his removal at a meeting of the Democratic Party. After it he was given the chance to shake up the Italian political system, because few days later he was formally sworn in, becoming, at the age of 39 the youngest Prime Minister in modern Italian history.

This was the first cabinet in which male and female ministers were present in equal numbers (the Prime Minister excluded). But would appointing a comparative youngster in a cabinet, the age of whose members averaged 47 make a real difference? And would Renzi survive the same political logjam that ultimately cost Letta his job? The Five Star Movement's leader, Beppe Grillo was scathing, suggesting that a dark coup had taken place and that Italian Democracy was fraying at the edges. Grillo also made the point that Letta had been the second prime minister in a row to take power without winning an election and that Renzi was now the third.

In early 2016 was Renzi was still the leader and since coming to office his government implemented numerous reforms, including a radical overhaul of the Italian Senate, numerous changes to the electoral system, a relaxation of labour and employment laws with the intention of boosting economic growth and the abolition of many small taxes.

In March 2018 there was a general election with the Five Star Movement winning the most seats. Unfortunately for them, they weren't enough to win an outright majority.

10 Public Statements

It was my turn to arrive late for the day's reunion around the fountain. I hadn't been for over three weeks because I'd had things to do, but because I'd been something of a regular, I felt obliged to attend. Having to listen to them lamenting about ageing bones, blocked arteries and pseudo-mythical sexual encounters, I was less keen than I had been to go. The repetition was drying me out and I'd begun to feel that attending now and again was enough, but my tardy appearance was not appreciated and I received some sarcastic digs from the boys. 'There are seven days in a week,' they told me, 'therefore there are seven reunions.' Lest I'd forgotten, Bruno, the retired waiter with the bushy white hair reminded me that aperitivi start at eleven hundred hours every morning.

When I first started going to the meetings I was greeted with broad smiles and enthusiastic handshakes. As a newcomer in a close community, this was pleasing for me and because of this welcome I could have believed I possessed an innate charm, or that I encouraged a pleasant greeting from these comparative strangers because I brought inspiring conversation. But, in time I figured out that it wasn't either of those reasons. It was because I was a good listener, somebody new to off-load their gripes, their concerns about their aches, and pains and to whom they could indulge in their personal foibles. I was somebody who gave them sympathy and pity, who tried his best to offer practical suggestions to help them overcome their trials and tribulations and as long as I did no more than that, I was welcome, but when I started going to the reunions for the same reasons that they went, their attitude towards me began to change. In contrast to the earlier gushing reception, when I went for a change of scenery and to read the daily newspaper and to have a drink, and not necessarily to provide the commiserative listening facility I'd been supplying, I started to receive the same inconsequential 'ciao' as they gave to each other. To accept me into their society and to call me a *bravo ragazzo* (a good boy) and not a *stronzo* (a shit) I discovered they had placed upon me certain preconditions, particularly a permanently bent ear, and if I didn't uphold them I would be cold-shouldered.

But let's put the size of this community, and this group into perspective. The population of Surrey, where Nicola and I used to live is around half a million and out of them I knew maybe one hundred people. The population of Argegno is just six hundred souls and I know nearly every one of them, and yet the old boys' collective persona seems much bigger in comparison to the relative size of the population. I've come to believe that instead of just me the boys would prefer a steady turnover of newcomers to their village upon whom they can inflict their complaints, because I think they are becoming jaded with me. 'Why,' they ask, 'when the average age of our pensioner population is seventy-five for men and seventy-nine for women, do you want to live here?' They could have a point. Sitting around with a pile of fogeys watching each day flitter away with no appreciable gain, if any is probably an inane thing to do. Whiling away the hours waiting for the Grim Reaper to make his selection can be all-pervasive and unless an individual chooses to throw in the towel, the aforementioned Harvester is not particularly fussy whom he collects. Some reckon he has been known to make mistakes, so increasing my distance from them could be a shrewd thing to do.

The inimitable Mario is having a moody this morning, which isn't surprising, because his daughter has wandered over from la *pasticceria* (the pastry shop), carrying a bag of cream cakes that she doesn't intend to share with anybody else. He remains seated, but she has to stand, because females are not allowed to join the group (which of course has total rights to the seat around the fountain). She has arrived to pester him for money and this is making him snarl. She is large and has bleached hair that looks like mouldy hay. She is thirty-six, unmarried and she has got to be the laziest person I've ever seen, because the only active things I've seen her do are yawn, scratch her head and eat cakes. It's clear she fancies me, even though I've never spoken to her so she's started to frequent the fountain, not only to mug her dad not only to mug her dad for money but also to ogle me. There's never any 'please' or 'thank you' from her when she's after his cash. She just stands in front of him, holding twitching fingers under his nose until he fills her hand with a satisfactory amount of euro notes, whilst she grins at him and winks at me.

Mario may think I'm a covert threat, come to take his life away. Telling him that I live on Lake Como to paint the landscape never seems to satisfy him and his suspicions about me grow. To give him cause for concern, I did tell him I was really here to marry his daughter as a way of getting my hands on his stash when he dies. He didn't think that was very funny, but his pals did. Mario must have thought I was serious about wanting to be related to him, and had told his daughter what I'd said, because for the last weeks she's started to dress like a

Barbie doll. If she thinks I'm looking at her, she'll jiggle her boobs at me. I have to admit, I do look at her, but out of dismay and disbelief rather than longing or lust.

The day's motion is the state of the European Union. Debate is fast flowing and before very long the boys decide it has become one enormous cause for dissatisfaction. They tell me that at its conception in the late 1950s they were under the impression that membership of the what was then the Common Market would be a cure for Italy's stagnation, that the system would shoulder her poor health and would change decades of inadequacy, but it hasn't happened. There's a lull in proceedings where we consider our disquieting future, but Guido grabs the lull by the collar and starts on about his semi-blindness again. He's spent most of his life reading literature and he is genuinely broken hearted because he is no longer able to do so. He has to rely on his wife to do it for him or for us to give him snippets of information from the newspapers. He's always asking us to read out "the good bits", but finding out what they are can be a subjective and tiring business.

A young Italian woman that none of us recognise passes by and this shakes us out of our mood. Naturally, Alessandro is the first to pipe up about the enormity of her breasts and we all laugh. They make calculations about the amount of liquid they hold and dispute whether it may not be milk, but an acceptable vino. Even Guido laughs and for a few seconds forgets he cannot see properly. Alessandro remarks on how Guido can see clearly enough when there's something worth looking at. In the end the morning turns out to be one of joviality, especially when a smiling antique in the form of Angelo arrives. None of us would have recognised him if it hadn't been for his familiar sticks, because he's just had a set of false teeth fitted and they make his face look much fatter and his smile much whiter. He's arrived to ask the committee for their opinion, but they are disconcerted, because every time he speaks he sprays spittle in all directions and we have to recoil to avoid being showered. He's seventy-seven years old and as he's been almost toothless for twenty years, his gums have shrunk. In return for his aquatic address, he's showered with remonstrations from his so-called mates and so he removes his top plate in an attempt to rectify matters. He starts making rolls of tissue to place inside the plates in the hope that the tissue will absorb the excessive moisture, but drops his top plate on the unremorseful stone pavement and it splits in two. He surrendered an insurance policy to pay for his new teeth and now they've been rendered useless.

One of us suggests superglue to fix them back together. Another says, 'Mama mia, for God's sake don't take the bottom set out!' We all laugh at his misfortune and, bless him so does he. Still, in compensation we now see the old Angelo we know and love and not the new, almost artificial one.

Angelo leaves and Enrico arrives. A few of the boys wriggle to one side to make a space for him so he can sit down, but he remains standing. He tells the ensemble he's not here for enjoyment, because he's far too preoccupied to idle the day away. I haven't seen him for months, and I'm told it's because his daughter has bought an apartment nearby and she's seconded him to do it up for her. It's become agony for him, because he never stops working on it. The group sympathises with him, but then one of them whispers to me, 'he doesn't know what he's doing.'

As if to prove it, Enrico produces a heavy looking plastic bag of IKEA furniture fittings. He cannot fathom them out and he's looking for volunteers to help him with them, so he can assemble the flat-pack furniture from which they came. Nobody raises a hand to offer help. He's looking worried, because his daughter wants to occupy the place in four weeks' time and its entire contents are waiting to be put together. So far it's taken him three days to assemble just one single wardrobe with sliding doors. In unison the group tries to persuade him to drown his sorrows, and to help him one of them has poured him a tumbler full of vino rosso, but he's still refusing to relax. Three minutes later he's on his way with a tear of desperation in the corner of his eye, because he hasn't found a volunteer.

To change the subject, Vittorio reads aloud from the day's *La Repubblica* newspaper about life threatening alterations to the governments pension legislation. It's enough to make Mario go loopy. Any news about pensions is a sensitive subject with the old boys. Some of them are much reliant on theirs and they don't trust the government anymore because they keep moving the goalposts. The peculiarity is, Mario is the richest person in the village and so the least needy, but he always makes the loudest noise if something about pensions comes up and it starts him off in a rant. If anybody wants to liven up proceedings and have a laugh at his expense, all they have to do is mention the word "pension" and he starts flinging things about. And just in case we didn't know already, he tells us yet again that he receives €8,300 per annum and he has to pay €1,153 in tax. It's as well the minister for labour and welfare is far away in Rome, because Mario has just issued him with threats of an obscene and tortuous nature, should he ever pass his house.

'Have you ever heard anything so crazy?' he continues. 'I worked alongside my wife in my restaurant for seventy-hours a week, for forty gruelling years. Like a fool I paid all my contributions to our wonderful government, and this is the pittance they give me in return. It's a humiliating disgrace!'

His mates almost feel sorry for him but it's not for his burdensome tax payments. It's for him having to work with his wife for seventy hours a week for forty years.

When I get my hands on the morning paper, I read to the gathering a letter in it, entitled, "The Flight of Young Talent." It says that the country is losing its most valuable resource and the reasons for this is because Italy hasn't changed its ways since the last wave of economic migrants departed a century ago. It also announces that fifty thousand Italians leave Italy each year in the hope of forging a career in Switzerland, Germany or Britain, but particularly Germany, where they are short of engineers, nurses and carers for the elderly. The Goethe Institute has never been so busy providing German lessons to Greek and Spanish as well as Italian migrants, so they can capitalise on the opportunities available in a fellow European country. The institute is also offering lessons in German culture, and in addition has launched technical language courses tailored to the needs of young migrant doctors, lawyers and engineers. To encourage people to stay in Italy, so the story says, the Italian government needs to create a climate in which new businesses can start up. Italy has had minimal growth in the last decade with Italians worse off on average than they were in 2003.

'What's different?' the old boys reply. 'What goes around comes around. It's only what we expected. We remember hardship when we were children. We wanted to leave the country then but we hadn't the means to do it.'

Another article draws attention to the near economic collapse, with Europe spending billions to keep the euro afloat. Added to which, echoes of what has gone on in Spain are now happening in Italy. The construction industry is facing collapse, leaving thousands of those gravity-defying tower cranes looming idly over constructions that will never be finished. Nor will they be demolished, because that would cost as much as finishing them. Tens of thousands of protesters - unionists, left-wing parties, teachers, workers and members of Italy's communist party - marched through Rome at the height of the summer season, united in protest against austerity. Some demonstrators wore giant devil masks, whilst others carried life-size puppets of Italian politicians and Angela Merkel, and vast banners saying "no more CUTS!" On the same day, in another part of Rome, twenty thousand medics, wearing white gowns and carrying banners with their messages appearing to be written in blood, demonstrated against cuts to the health service. On live television the labour and welfare minister shed tears as she announced an increase in the retirement age. At the same time the government announced an increase in IVA (the equivalent of the UK's Value Added Tax) from twenty-one per cent to twenty-three per cent.

A new old boy has arrived from a neighbouring village to see his Argegnini comrades. 'Michele!' they all cry in a welcoming unison. 'Come stai (how are you)?'

I've never met him before, nor have I heard anybody mention his name. He seems bright and friendly. He's arrived dressed in the accepted smart-casual uniform of short-sleeved, impeccably pressed white shirt, although his is not unbuttoned to the second button because he has a blue tie attached to the snug fitting collar. Below, however he has the obligatory perfectly creased light grey trousers and polished black slip-on shoes.

He is a big man with big hands. He also has a large face with a hooked nose, tinted with the blue veins of a drinker, as if it had been designed specifically to dip into the glass of Barbera he's just been handed. Maybe that is how it became blue, or maybe the reason for a Roman nose is to differentiate the connoisseur from the proletarian? He takes in the bouquet, raises his glass to the sky to both check its depth of colour and to salute us all and downs it in one.

As Michele is pouring himself another glass, he's introduced to me by Pino, who tells me he is an ex-hotel employee and barman and he speaks English like a native of Scotland. He was about to take a seat, but he raises himself up again to greet me when he hears I am English. It proves he is courteous as well as having an obliging disposition and his reaction is to try his English on me. I recognise a hint of a Scottish brogue, but then he acknowledges in Italian that his English is very rusty, so I mustn't expect too much. He reveals he married an Edinburgh girl when he was working in Edinburgh. Then, he tells me he spent some years working in Glasgow in the 1960s, but only in the top hotels and in a selection of some whisky bars selling the finest Island single malts. He returned to his family home twenty years ago when his wife died. He's eager to continue with his story, but because his mates haven't seen him for some time they demand his attention and he doesn't get another chance to practice his English. He is then whisked away to the other side of the fountain, where most of the wine is being drunk and I can only hear what the general conversation is about by leaning sideways. It appears he's been offered a good price for his house by a building developer, who wants the land for a block of four luxury apartments. His mates don't know if they should be pleased or not, so they wait to hear that Michele seems happy with the price. It will certainly supplement his state pension, so they are glad for him. But his heart is sad, he tells them because he will have to leave his beloved medieval home to live somewhere he's not interested in, so they change their tone to one of commiseration. Although this will make him money, he knows the new-build will change the physical look of his village. It seems he's about to sell his soul to materialism and run away with the money on offer. He knows it's a moral dilemma, but he's not the first to be tempted.

It's turning out to be a morning of surprises for the boys, because Albano, a chirpy chappie who is seldom seen has turned up. Physically, he is a complete contrast to Michele, because he is tiny, but he too is dressed elegantly and he is eager for a drink and a chat. Out of his earshot, Vittorio informs me that at one time, Albano was a lot richer than Mario. He was an olive grower and oil bottler - he even has a complexion not unlike a ripe olive - and for decades he supplied the local area with the precious liquid. That was, until he spent a two year spell in the clink for defrauding the European Union Subsidy Board of half a million euro. His demise came about when the bureaucrats in Brussels became very unhappy with him claiming agricultural grants for olive trees he didn't have. And he almost got away with it.

On the few occasions I have seen Albano, he has always been outgoing and is always laughing. I wouldn't be surprised if he was laughing when he was arrested for swindling the Subsidy Board. He has a tongue-in-cheek attitude towards most things, especially towards the olive trees he never had. The story goes he produced then presented the EU Commission for Agriculture a map that was over a century old. It had been drawn when his grandfather was alive, when the area of land the family olive farm covered was a lot larger than it is on a modern map. He then altered the present day map to include the land and the number of trees the family once owned in his grandfather's day, then forwarded a copy to Brussels, thereby for ten years claiming a subsidy of €50 per olive tree per year for trees that no longer existed.

Albano, like Michele, speaks a bit of English, but only a bit, because he tells me he spent a year working in Birmingham as a youth. And as if to justify his claim he asks me if I know any dirty English jokes, because he says they are the best. I don't have any but I said I'd download some off the Internet and then translate them for him. 'Can you do it by tomorrow?' he asks. 'Because I'm only in Argegno infrequently and we might never meet again.'

During the conversation with Albano, the same young lady with the outstanding figure that walked past us the other day walks past again and once again we all admire her. To remind him of his association with England, I turn to him and say, 'what a lovely pair of Bristols she's got!'

I thought he'd understand the remark, but he doesn't and insists I explain it. I say it is an English joke. As soon

as I say "joke", he is all ears and is even more insistent. I
Then have to explain rhyming slang to him and he doesn't
understand that either. I ask him if he's heard of a city in
England called Bristol. 'Of course I have,' he replies. 'It's
just along the M5 from Birmingham, where I used to
work. But what has that got to do with the outstanding
breasts the girl is carrying before her?'

I laughed and so does he. I'm laughing out of irony
because I don't know how to finish what I'd just started,
but I didn't know why he was laughing. He is looking at
me as if he is asking me why I'm laughing. So, once again I
attempt to explain rhyming slang. 'It's a form of wit,' I say,
'where you replace a common word or expression with a
phrase that rhymes with it, that has nothing to do with the
original. For instance, Bristol is a city in England and they
have a football team called Bristol City. In Britain, breasts
are vulgarly called "titties". So, in rhyming slang they
become a pair of "Bristol Cities", abbreviated to
"Bristols."

'Si, si, capito (yes, yes, now I have understood),' he said.

An hour later he is still sitting next to me, when the
same woman walks past the fountain for the second time
that day. The buoyant Albano claps his eyes on her once
again, gives me a sharp nudge in the ribs, jumps to his feet,
points directly at her and in perfect English, shouts, 'what
a lovely pair of Birminghams she's got!'

Enrico returns, looking bamboozled. He is also
worried, because he has far less time to complete his
daughter's apartment than he first told us. He spreads a
sheet of IKEA furniture instructions on the bench next to
Albano and puts a full glass of wine on each of the four
corners to weigh it down. He prepares himself to implore
us to take a look at a confusion of self-assembly
instructions. When he believes he's got our full attention
he says he cannot believe the expectations that IKEA must
have of their customers, expecting them to construct a

suite of bedroom furniture that he reckons was designed at the NASA space laboratory. Alessandro isn't interested in the furniture, so from the football page of the newspaper he's reading he reveals (to those that didn't know already), that Juventus lost at home to lowly Siena last night in the Italian Cup. Mario's passion for Juvé holds no bounds and he was hoping that nobody would notice the catastrophic result the paper has reported. He should be so lucky. The *Milanesti*, the AC Milan supporters, and the *Internazionale*, the Inter Milan supporters, sitting on the other side of the fountain are too malicious to let the opportunity to slag off a rival supporter go to waste. So, with Alessandro's assistance, they scour the back page for nuggets of information to hammer home the point and they give Mario a torrid five minutes. But it's not yet over and they move into sensitive territory, switching to allegations about Juvé's alleged match-fixing scandal, including paying referees to make sure they don't lose.

Mario had been hoping to escape the torment his so-called mates are dishing out. Mario is a monster when he's riled. He's looking at his rival *tifosi* (fans) menacingly from the corners of his eyes but he doesn't move his head to face their abuse. His eyebrows are twitching, which isn't a good sign. He's a cat, poised, keeping perfectly still until the second is ripe to pounce. Knowing Mario like we all do, he would undoubtedly like to be standing over their open graves, urinating on their coffins, but instead his intention is to dissolve the argument about his team his way and his constrained force is about to explode all over the piazza. With four glasses of bianco sporco drunk on an empty stomach, and the pension saga still simmering, he comes back at their taunt with aggression. In a vain attempt to protect his tenuous dignity, he hurls back some hurtful snarls about them not having lawful fathers. It leaves them smouldering. For the rest of us it's just a bit of fun to see him reeling under fire and a few of the old boys join in the slagging match, adding more insults to fire him up. According to Mario, not only are modern day soccer stars a bunch of overpaid mercenaries who hold no commitment or loyalty to their fans or their fat contracts, but they too arrived on this earth with questionable parentage. He's now so worked-up his face has gone puce in colour. Now he's fusing his two immediate concerns together, his earlier threat of violence to the labour and welfare minister now includes lining-up all Seria A footballers alongside the entire ministerial cabinet in the Senate and flogging the lot of them, then to start afresh with an honest brood.

One of the boys shouts to a barman who has been witnessing the kerfuffle from the other side of the piazza, demanding he supply us with a round of chilled white wine and some slices of pizza as quick as he can. Having done so we manage to calm Mario down for the good of his delicate health, with the promise that there is a restorative on its way. None of us wants his wife to blame us for killing him, when or if she returns from Australia, because she is a battle-axe and if she believed we had, she would probably attempt to kill us as well.

Vittorio is a calming influence on Mario and as the tray of drinks arrives he brings up a new subject to take Mario's mind off his obsessions. The subject, the amount of *conservante* (preservatives) in wine was surely already on his agenda and he asks for his comrades' analysis. This is another topic that never gets resolved, but it seems to bring Mario back to his senses. They all agree that wine bought directly from la cantina (the vine producer) is the purest and safest. It makes sense to buy it before any preservatives are added for long term bottling, and it tastes the best. The snag is the nearest cantina that sells it is in the Valtelina. This is a three-hour drive, there and back, so to make the journey worthwhile, they would have to buy a lot of vino, and then there is the problem of storing it properly. Vittorio is all for it. He tells them he has the use of his son's truck this coming weekend, so they could collect hundreds of litres of the fine liquid in fifty four-litre demijohns, those huge glass vessels with fat bodies and slender necks, enclosed in plaited wicker baskets. It has to be a team effort to collect and transport it, with the booze divided amongst the group or it's not cost effective. Regardless of this, no one raises a hand to volunteer to take part in such an expedition. The main obstacle preventing the decision is that vino without conservante has to be drunk within a year of the racking process or it starts to turn to vinegar, and they are unwilling to commit to such an investment if they are unsure of capitalising on it by drinking it all in time. The opportunity to do something positive, instead of being slowly poisoned by commercial wine, comes to nothing. In the end they reject Vittorio's offer because they don't want to be forced into drinking the same wine every day of the year to get rid their quota before it goes off, even if it is better for them.

11 Bel Paese

The lake is swelling tonight; unlike its usual placid state, it is swishing around. The moon hangs against a cobalt-blue sky with a distinct glass orb with a touch of madder-red mixed into it. Its gravity is so forceful that it makes the water vibrate. This electrifying sight is complemented by the silhouettes of the tall, speckled, plane trees on the short promenade. These giants too are restless, waving their arms as they sway in time with the swell of the water. They make an eerie, though not alarming creaking sound in the autumn air, as if calling for their lost bark to be returned. But they are not the only things swaying under the October sky.

I have spied the silhouette of another gigantic form close by. It is Fabio. He is meandering, almost out of control down the centre of the lakeside road and appears to be heading in my direction. He is dressed in a grimy, brightly patterned short-sleeved shirt and equally grimy navy blue shorts. Fabio is not one of the old boys; he's forty-seven. He's a two-metre high builder's mate, built like a brick privy, with an unruly mop of ginger hair that is usually covered in brick dust. When he scratches his head, a red cloud forms around him.

Fabio was one of the first people we met when we came to live in Italy. He was a renowned member of the local rowing club, having rowed in the double-sculls for Italy in the 1988 Seoul Olympics, where he won a bronze medal. I like Fabio a lot, but he drinks too much and when he does he becomes reckless with his money. He's often found combing the villages around the lake, looking for somebody he knows to share a drink with. When he does, he will insist on paying for everything. When we lived in Moltrasio I made the error of getting involved with him on too many occasions, but since we moved to Argegno I've managed to evade most, if not all of his offers. My last lapse took place about a year before, in the Bar Onda. My main memory of that fateful incident was the first half-hour in his company, where he taught me how to lay imaginary bricks in the middle of the bar floor. And after sinking half a dozen glasses of *bianco sporco* (literally, "dirty white" - white wine with Campari soda) it was blotto time and I lost count of how many more we downed and how many bricks I was supposed to have lain.

If Fabio happens to be around Argegno and he spies me, he uses the only two English words he knows - 'you drink?' I'm sure that Fabio targets me because he's got it in his head that all Brits are alike, especially when they are on holiday. His impression has been reinforced by television documentaries that display the British tendency for alcohol-fuelled hooliganism. As hard as I try to convince him that I drink a maximum of two small bottles of beer or half a bottle of wine a day, and that I am not a twelve pint a day man like the stereotypical Brit, it makes no difference.

Part of the reason why the Brits indulge so much when they are abroad is because booze is half the price it is in the UK. The quantity they drink amazes not only Fabio, but all Italians. He's told me several times that he always enjoys the company of Brits, especially when he tries to out-drink them. Fabio must think I'm a bit flaky, and I'm sure he's not altogether convinced I am English, because I don't drink anywhere near the amount he believes I ought.

Fabio is the strongest person I've ever met, and to prove it, when he's had a few drinks he will pick a person up by the elbows and lift their feet off the ground. I weigh ninety kilos and he can pick me up as if I were a bag of popcorn. He owns an old Lambretta scooter and when he rides it he never wears a crash helmet or uses his lights. This is common practice in Italy for locals who travel short distances, but one night he was knocked off his scooter by a hit-and-run driver in a very long tunnel. He then walked three kilometres to the nearest bar, where he drowned the pain he was feeling. He then worked for three weeks before admitting to himself that he had a broken ankle.

I'm still down by the lake and it definitely looks as if Fabio is heading my way, so I think it's safest to hide behind the fattest tree trunk I can find. I am timing his approach. As he closes in, I circle the opposite way around the tree. He had obviously seen me, but because he's as drunk as a rat, I'm praying he'll think he'd imagined seeing me and pass by. Because he is so affable, it's unkind to avoid him, but I want him to save his money rather than squander it. Also, I only need him in small doses and not the excessive alcoholic one he will insist on pouring into me if he does find me.

He's arrived at the spot where I was when I saw him approaching. He is swaying as he looks around. Only his size fifteen, steel toecapped, cement-covered boots keep him upright. He's staggering past at this very second. He's so close I can smell the brick dust in his hair and the odour of warm wine that clings to his clothes. He's within touching distance, but he's not found me and he's shaking his head in puzzlement. Now he's moving towards the ornamental railings that surround the lake and he's leaning over them precariously. He must think I've fallen into the water. He's still leaning over the railings and calling my name at the same time. 'Paul, dove sei?' 'Paul, where are you?' Fortunately he looks like he's given up trying to find me and instead is trying to remember his bearings.

Phew, that was close.

He's now attempting to cross the road to piazza Roma where the bars are, but instead of taking the forty-five degree angle he needs to take to get there he's meandering way off course. At this time of night his state of inebriation is notorious; it's the same scene, on the same stretch of road, at the same time of night, seven nights a week. Motorists slow almost to a stop to give him space in case they crash into him and he damages their cars, but he passes on, insensible, to reappear where we least expect him.

~~~

One morning at the fountain, Mario leaned his face away from the glass of wine he was holding and asked me if I was going on the annual mangialonga the next day. It would take place way above Argegno in the Intelvi mountain villages and would include plates and plates of indigenous food so I was booked myself in to go: Nicola and I had been on similar events but it was my first time for this particular one. Nicola was away, working in Rome, but even if she had been around, she wouldn't have gone, because she cannot pack away the amount of food a person is expected to pack away (or at the rate they pack it away) and she is often staggered at how they do it.

"Mangialonga" means, "long eat" and it is a greedy person's dream but the Intelvi one turned out to be different from others; Usually there is a bus laid on to take the participants from venue to venue, but in this one everyone gets some exercise between the several courses of meat, polenta, pasta, risotto, cheeses, roast chestnuts, huge sticky deserts, caffè, and an unlimited amount of wine by walking from one venue to the next. It is something of an endurance test, both of an individual's stomach capacity and their legs, because although the walks between the destinations are not in themselves hard, they certainly feel that way when carrying a heavily laden belly around.

The price of the *ghita* (the trip) was €35 per head and it started in the village of San Fedele. Most of the forty people who had booked had been going on it for years. They would meet up at a bar at 10am for a light breakfast that includes an espresso coffee mixed with a shot of grappa or cognac and a brioche, then walk from one eating or drinking establishment to another, in a succession of villages, over a distance of five kilometres. It is a highly sociable affair, as all Italian events are, and as we walk and talk in a group or in pairs we soon find ourselves at the next epicurean spot. The itinerary has a fairly strict timetable, and the leader and organiser of the event, in this case a local builder, will tell us all how long we have to eat or drink in each place before we have to move onto the next one. This can be anything from half an hour to two hours. It finishes in Cerano around five o'clock in the afternoon as it starts to get dark, and then we are supposed to walk back to the starting point in the San Fedele bar, where we say our farewells with a promise to repeat the joyful outing the following year.

As I said before, these events are beyond Nicola. When she is faced with a pizza in an Italian restaurant I always have to finish it for her. To her it seems that Italians, especially the women eat the quantities they do on mangialonge as if by magic, and she always wants to know where they put it and how they still manage to remain so thin. Statistically, Italians are among the slimmest people in the world, with only ten per cent of the population in the obesity range, so she is puzzled as to how that can be, when they break all the rules by eating pasta, bread, cakes and desserts. Although Nicola's character has become more Italian than English since we've lived here, I sometimes ask her why we are living here, because she isn't that interested in food, when, at least thirty per cent of an Italian's life, either male or female involves the preparation and the consumption of a meal, and when it is over and cleared away, the planning starts for the next one. These days, the stereotypical large meals that Italians are famous for are only enjoyed on special occasions. On some of these occasions a meal can take three or four hours to consume. It is not unknown in this region for a group of men on an outing to consume three pizzas each, with the one who cannot force the last mouthful down having to pick up the tab. But usually, Italians eat less food, and much lighter courses at home than in a restaurant. Not many Italians have breakfast. As we have seen with our two imbianchini, it is not considered the most important meal of the day - an espresso is sufficient. Breakfast cereals are a recent addition to the Italian diet and usually bought for the children. Before that, a child's breakfast consisted of un' panino (a bread roll from the day before), broken into pieces and served in a bowl of warm milk.

Lunch and dinner are sit-down meals, with portions of a reasonable size and well balanced. The first course is likely to be either spaghetti in tomato sauce, gnocchi with pesto, a small portion of ravioli or other filled pasta or a bowl of soup. The second course will be a moderate portion of fish, poultry or veal with a couple of vegetable side dishes. The meal will finish with a green salad, dressed with virgin olive oil and balsamic vinegar. Often at the table there will be a bowl of good olives and a basket of bread rolls, but no butter. Italians tend not to snack and usually only drink alcohol with a meal (although our old boys are exceptions to this!). This is usually red wine, taken in moderation, along with bottled mineral water. The main course of an evening meal can be grilled, roasted or stewed meat or fish. In mountainous areas, traditional stews with fresh herbs are popular and in the winter especially, game with polenta. Some homes have a wood-fired grill or a brick oven just outside the kitchen to cook steaks, chicken fillets and sausages. In other households, if the family has eaten a largish meal at lunchtime they will eat from a tray of cheeses, sliced meats, olives and fruit and mixed nuts instead of a cooked evening meal.

Both lunch and dinner are unhurried, accompanied by plenty of conversation. People linger at the table and after lunch is over they will take a rest before returning to work. After dinner they may take a stroll for an hour or so and stop at a bar for a light drink, and maybe a dessert, which will generally contain less sugar than those of other countries. Light exercise seems to be enough for city dwellers. People shop nearly every day, and walk to the shops because in the smaller towns and villages most things they require are a short distance away.

I love Italian food and I can eat almost anything that is presented to me (the exception being Italian frogs), but Nicola continues to have problems, saying Italians are obsessed with eating. Her proclivity is to eat when she's hungry, not because food is readily available. I hoped she'd become more accustomed to the eating culture the longer she was here, but the reverse seems to be the case: apart from vegetables, cheese, eggs and a tiny amount of pasta it is difficult to think of anything else she'll go for. She doesn't like meat, especially when she cannot tell what part of the animal it comes from, and most certainly will not eat offal. She dislikes fish even more than meat and that seems a wasted opportunity, especially as we live right next to a vast lake that is teeming with fish. Despite the fact that the majority of the dishes of the region contain meat of some sort, Nicola remains ninety per cent vegetarian. She is an animal lover and when she sees things like pig's heads, trotters, tripe, cocks-combs, horsemeat, donkey meat or sheep's brains for sale she goes pale. The thought of eating pig's ears or worse, the pig snouts in the traditional *cassoeula* makes her turn a little faint. She tells me, and lots of Italians she knows, that when she reads certain menus, especially ones advertising local country fare, she visualises gruesome pictures of animals in her mind's eye that she cannot bear. *Cotoletta alla Milanese* evokes an image of a calf being breadcrumbed and deep-fried. A rabbit stew conjures images of little fluffy things being stripped of their flesh. If she sees sliced donkey meat on a butchers slab, she sees Daniele's animals grazing in his fields and spit roasted venison with gravy makes her turn away. Of all animals, Nicola's main love is horses and if she sees horsemeat for sale or on somebody's plate she'll say *'che schifo'* - it's disgusting. She won't even eat horseradish sauce, because it's got the name horse in it. When she goes on a mangialonga, the rest of party wonder why she bothers turning up if she intends passing on three-quarters of the menu. And the concept of vegetarianism is a mystery to most Italians, and some of them have said to her, 'Se non vi piace carne, quindi provare il salame invece (if you don't like meat, try the salami instead).'

Every region in Italy has developed its own culinary talents and Italians think only in terms of their own regional cuisine, with each town or village adding its own unique touch to a dish. A lot of game is eaten locally. Nothing of a slaughtered animal or bird is wasted, so Nicola tries not to look at the food, preferring instead to drink the wine. I've tried telling her to put her horrific images to the back of her mind, at least for the duration of a meal if we are in a restaurant or at a festa but she says she wishes she could!

She dreads being invited to people's homes to eat, in case she is asked to witness what in her eyes is a murder scene. If she can't turn down an invitation, it has been known for her to pretend to be eating, especially if there is red meat on her plate. She will cut it into little pieces then arrange it around her plate in an attempt to make it look as though she's eating it, although very little of it will actually reach her mouth. Then, when or if the host leaves the room she will quickly slide it onto my plate to save her embarrassment, but if she is stuck in a situation when the host doesn't leave the room, when the time comes to clear away her plate she will tell them that she is full up and couldn't eat another thing.

If Nicola thinks she is about to receive an invitation from somebody she presupposes is a big meat eater, she will get her invite in first, thereby changing the location to our villa so she can offer them something she herself will enjoy. The problem here is they are likely to be hesitant about accepting her invite because we are English. More than likely they will have heard some terrible stories about English cuisine, or they may have visited England and had bad experiences, so they will be unsure as to what they will receive and diplomatically will ask us just what it is the English eat. What they really mean is, 'before we accept your invitation we'd like a run-through of the intended menu, just in case we have to invent an excuse not to turn up.'

The problem we have here is, compared to Italian food, there is precious little we can tell them about what is a typically English dish. Famous English dishes like bacon and eggs, fish and chips, shepherd's pie or Cornish pasties aren't right for an evening meal, nor for that matter is a Sunday roast if it's not a Sunday. And certainly not a curry (which of course isn't actually English in origin, but happens to be the most eaten dish in the UK). After that, it starts to get a bit problematic as to what is actually English, apart from the standard bangers and mash, toad in the hole, bubble and squeak, spotted dick or gooseberry fool, but translating a description of these dishes is likely to scare them off. But they needn't worry, because Nicola is a brilliant cook. Her specialities are always Italian and more often than not the meat they will find on their plates will be minced beef in a ragu or lasagne. She's also touchy about eating chicken. Chicken breast is acceptable but legs, gizzards, wings and combs are not and if she has decided we are going to eat chicken, I will have to prepare it for the pot because she cannot bear to touch raw flesh. She actually likes liver pâté, but if it were served to her as sliced liver she would shudder at it. Fortunately, from experience she knows what will be acceptable to our Italian guests, and so far none of them have left dissatisfied. In fact, most of them have passed genuine compliments to her on her outstanding Italian cooking, especially her polenta, because her recipe includes four different cheeses and it is the best they'll taste in the region. Her lake fish or seafood is also very good and although she cannot swallow it herself, she cooks it to perfection, usually in a good white wine or cider.

The majority of Italians refuse to try recipes with which they are unfamiliar, deciding they don't like them before they've even tried them. A lot of Italians will not travel abroad because they have heard about some culinary experiences they know they would feel uncomfortable with. A lot will not even travel around Italy, never mind abroad, especially to the south because what southerners eat is noticeably different from the northern diet and *vice versa*. Some northerners describe southern food as *schifezza* (filth) whilst some southerners say northern food is as boring and as bland as the people.

Nicola enjoys telling Italians a story she recalls about English food. A few years ago she accompanied a group of fourteen Italian businessmen from Milan on a trade mission to Coventry. The group wanted to try a typical English meal for the first time. They were bemused to discover there were no English restaurants serving English food. There were plenty of Indian, Italian, Chinese, Thai, Greek and Mexican restaurants and a few sushi bars, but none - certainly in Coventry - were advertising themselves as English. So, one evening, instead of them eating Italian every time, she asked the hotel they were staying in to come up with something typically English. The first course was oxtail soup, which Nicola said was received well. The other courses were served by waitress service, from trolleys, one part of the course at a time, over the shoulder of each diner. The main course was roast beef, with roast potatoes, sliced carrots, Brussels sprouts, parsnips and Yorkshire pudding. Piling everything on the plate is unknown in Italy, as is brown gravy, which was poured over the meat last. As each guest's plate was being filled, Nicola watched their faces for some enlightening expressions. Half of the fourteen looked enthralled, while the other half looked alarmed. There was a slight pause before starting, because a waitress was offering each person a tablespoonful of cranberry sauce on top of their dinner. This too is unknown in Italy and the person sitting next to Nicola, who had been particularly engrossed with what he had in front of him, said to her, 'Mio Dio, ha messo marmellata su di esso (My God, she's put jam on it as well)!'

But back to the mangialonga: we had spent half an hour having a ten o'clock colazione in a bar in the centre of the village, and the event finally got under way with us stepping across the road to another bar for a couple of glasses of a white Valtelline Superiore and a slice or two of *Sbrisolona*, a typical Lombardo cake, layered with a sweet lactic cheese and topped with Nutella. After that there was a fairly long hike to the village of Castigilone, to a trattoria where we ate *tortelli di zucca* (Ravioli filled with pumpkin), barbecued chicken drumsticks, polenta Valtellinese mixed with funghi porcini and Taragana cheese, accompanied by a half bottle each of Nino Negri and a half bottle of Nebbiolo.

Around mid-day, we went to another trattoria on the outskirts of the same village to try their tripe in broth with mixed chopped vegetables, then risotto alla Milanese (the only liquid used to cook the rice was Berlucchi spumante), with saffron and grated Grana Padano cheese, plus a selection of some of principle wines of Lombardy, just about all of which we sampled at one time or another during the day.

After that, we walked to Blessagno a tiny village with a population of two hundred and thirty seven. Here, at another trattoria we enjoyed a starter of fresh lake trout, followed by a choice of either cassoeula served with polenta or osso buco (braised shin of veal in a vegetable sauce), with wild porcini mushrooms fresh from the mountains and chopped celery, also served with polenta.

Around three o'clock we went to a restaurant further up the mountain where we had *Cotoletta alla Milanese* (veal cutlets coated in breadcrumbs) with chips, followed by cheese: Gorgonzola on crackers; the soft local cheese, Quartirolo Lombardo and Bitto, an alpine cheese from the Valtellina. For dessert we sampled panettone, a sweet dessert cake with a coating of icing sugar, served with mascarpone laced with Marsala. The wine included Grumello, Bonarda and grappa, plus caffè.

To finish off, in the late afternoon we gathered in the small village of Cerano, where a castagna festival was about to get under way. Castagne, are sweet chestnuts that grow prolifically in this area and are regarded as integral to the local diet and they are delicious. They are gathered as they fall and are eaten in several ways. On this day they were cooked on a griddle on an open fire, with the skin first pierced with a knife blade, to prevent them from exploding. In October into November there are castagna festivals in all the villages to celebrate the harvest, and the locals will gather round industrial sized grills to sample the year's crop, and as they do, they will wash it down with a few glasses of a dry Prosseco from the Veneto, together with large slices of panettone.

When it was all over we were supposed to walk back to the starting point in San Fedele, but I couldn't walk another step and I admit to cheating. It wasn't the food that had defeated me but the quantity of Bonarda, a slightly *frizzante* (sparkling) red wine I had drunk. So when I saw Fabio, the builder's mate with the sticky-out ginger hair approaching on his scooter I thumbed a lift to where my car was parked. As usual, he was without a crash helmet and when I asked him if he had a spare crash helmet for me, the ludicrousness of the question produced one of his bellowing laughs; so loud I was afraid it would draw attention to us. My only safeguard in begging for a lift was in knowing that if the police spotted us, his infamy as a drinker would encourage them to wave us past rather than stop us. As he travels within a ten-kilometre radius of his home for work purposes or to the nearest bar, they let him go because they see him as only a threat to himself. If they did pull him over, they'd need to arrest him every time, because he is permanently over the limit.

Until comparatively recently, it wasn't compulsory in Italy for the rider or passenger of a motorbike or a scooter with a capacity of 125cc or less to wear a crash helmet, but Fabio isn't interested in the law as he continues on his way, and if anybody asks him why he doesn't wear one he'd tell them he can't find one that fits. This could be true because his head, like his body, is something like an XXXL. However, it might help if he had his hair cut from time to time.

Fabio apart, Italians are moderate drinkers and they will generally not drink on an empty stomach. The majority don't touch a drop without having a snack or a meal in front of them. Red wine is considered more beneficial than white, especially when eating because it helps the digestion by breaking down fat in the gut. Bars are open all hours of the day and most of them close late, but to see a drunkard tottering around the streets is a rarity and would be considered as a *brutta figura* (an ugly figure). In Italy, even mild intoxication is regarded as bad manners, so some of the more puritanical villagers avoid Fabio like the plague. But the rest of the villagers like him because he is not the self-pitying type of drinker, nor is he the type who becomes moody or aggressive; in fact, he is quite the opposite. When he's sober he's happy and when he's had a few he's even happier and he can be good company. I try to avoid him, because although I enjoy having a laugh with him, he tries to tie me into a drawn out drinking session I cannot get away from. However, the local barmen welcome his company at all times, because he helps to keep them in business.

Being a Sunday it was Fabio's day off work, but of course it was not a day off from drinking. Although he wasn't officially on our outing, he seemed to be involved in it. As the main group walked and talked their way on the footpaths from one village and from one bar or trattoria to the next, he would be riding his scooter in the road, at the same time keeping up with us, joining in conversations en route and arriving at the same places to enjoy a drink. Apart from acknowledging him I didn't have the opportunity to chat to him much, but I noticed that when we sat down to eat in a trattoria he wasn't there. According to Pino's wife, he does the same thing every year. He looks forward to the outing as much as the people who have paid to be on it, but he never eats anything. Nevertheless, after we'd finished eating and it was time for us to walk to the next destination, he would be sitting on his scooter in the road, waiting to accompany us.

Fabio's scooter is an ancient, rusting Lambretta from the 1970s, and with a giant of a man like him on board it struggles to reach 40kph. He must weigh 120kg, and with me, at 90kg on the back, the poor scooter reached less than half of that speed on the way to San Fedele. It was a risk, but we were 1,000 metres above sea level and I'd never seen a policeman in the wilds of the Intelvi mountains. I just needed a lift for the last two kilometres to carry me to my car, because almost literally I was on my knees. Ten minutes was all the journey would take but as I cocked my leg over the pillion seat, I realised that my car was parked outside the bar where the event had begun and I knew it wasn't in Fabio's makeup to pass a bar, especially if he is in the company of someone he knows who owes him a favour for giving him a lift on his scooter. So, it would be my duty to provide him with a few drinks before he'd let me be on my way. The bigger risk was my driving home after a session with him. If I did get pulled over, the police would be unlikely to let me go, because they don't know me.

If I've had a drink and if the police are around, then I might try to make myself as insignificant as possible, because they are not renowned for conciliation or arbitration if there's the smell of alcohol coming from whoever is sitting behind a steering wheel. Although this is the state of affairs in most parts of the world, in Italy it seems the law keepers are more tolerant if they know you. I cannot guarantee this, but it appears from what I've witnessed that the local police are lenient when it comes to apprehending somebody they have known since they were boys together, and unless there has been an accident they tend to let the offender go. In recent years there has been a tightening up on the drink driving laws, but they do seem to turn a blind eye if a local event is happening and a number of people are likely to be driving home after they have had a few. But just in case the police weren't feeling affable, I took a back road through the village of Schignano that farmer Daniele had advised me to take if I had been a bit worse for wear after drinking his home made Barbera.

12 In America

"In America" is an expression Italians use to describe a life of plenty, when for instance an Italian has had a lucky break that has enabled him to make money and have an easy life. It undoubtedly stems from the time when boatloads of Italians crossed the Atlantic with the intention of making it big. A series of coincidences happened within the space of six months that would eventually take me to the USA, keeping me away from my studio in Argegno and the fountain in piazza Roma for some time.

It started with an attempt to do some rebuilding on our villa. The first floor had an open terrace of a hundred square metres, extending several metres under the slab between it and the floor above, to the back of the building. I wanted to turn this area into an art studio and office by closing it in with double-glazed sliding doors, leaving a terrace in front of the glass the same width as those on the upper floors. There was some urgency, because since we'd moved from Moltrasio I'd been using the boiler-cum-laundry room on the ground floor as a studio. This wasn't ideal, so we went to the Municipio to ask for planning permission to have the work done. It was necessary to declare this extra living space; if a property is altered, the rateable value may be changed and as I'd planned to make an extra room, the chances were that the rateable value would increase as well. Some people avoid the increase in taxation by not applying for permission, but if they are caught, the authorities can make them demolish what they have built or impose a large fine. If it remains undetected it doesn't mean they have got away with it completely, because if or when they come to sell their property, the intended purchaser's *Notaio* (Notary) contacts the Municipio for the land registry documents, and if he finds an extension that hasn't been declared, then permission to sell can be refused by the Municipio, and it will also be labelled *abusivo* (illegal).

To receive permission to erect the glass doors we needed to make an appointment with the *comune geometra* (community surveyor). After studying the original plans of the villa for ten minutes he told us that, because of its location we couldn't do it. This was a blow, because one of the reasons we had bought the villa was because I had hoped I could turn this area into an extra room at a moderate cost. All it needed to turn it into an ideal art studio and office space besides the double-glazed sliding doors were plaster on the walls, power points and lighting.

We couldn't understand why permission was refused, and when we asked why, the geometra said that it would create unsightly volume in an area of outstanding beauty. For a second or so I thought he must have misunderstood what we wanted to do, so I told him that the terrace already existed and all we wanted to do was to add a line of sliding glass doors and windows, and that was all that anybody was likely to see. How would that create volume? He still would not give way; in fact he looked at me as if I was some sort of troublemaker, and I had to bite my lip in case the meeting became heated. When we got back home, Nicola said she thought we might be being discriminated against. After all, only two hundred metres up the road there was a massive eight-apartment condominium being built, so how was that for creating volume? Also, two hundred metres in the other direction from our villa, a voluminous four-floor lift tower had just been added to the outside a house, creating far more volume than our proposed twelve-metre run of glass doors. It seemed ridiculous for him not to grant us permission. The whole of the lakeside was almost a building site, with new builds going up in every village. In Argegno alone, fifty new dwellings had been added in the past five years, and some of them were enormous constructions. If that wasn't "creating volume", then we didn't know what was.

A few weeks and a lot of grumbles later we tried again and this time we employed an independent local geometra to apply for permission. He drew some plans and "before and after" images of the first floor project and presented them to the comune geometra. We thought this would do the trick, not only because he is well known in the area and he knew the comune geometra, but also more importantly he knew the required jargon and the correct legislation. So, it was a case of waiting for the end of the month, when the comune decision makers, including the mayor, have their meeting to discuss new planning applications.

Still the local geometra wouldn't grant permission, citing the rules on volume. It seemed we had been unlucky in our choice of village and perhaps we should have lived somewhere else, because comune in other villages appeared to be giving permission for the kind of thing we were asking for. It all seemed so unjust, so we asked our geometra to check if there might have been discrimination against us. He told us that this particular council geometra goes by the book and he acts the same with Italians as he does with foreigners. 'I've tried every angle to get around the legislation,' he told us, 'but unless it changes, which may not happen in the near future then you cannot make any additions. Legally.' He stressed the word "legally", following it with the Italian equivalent of a 'nudge-nudge, wink-wink.'

Before we employed our geometra, we'd spoken to friends and neighbours in the area, telling them about the glacial response we'd received from the comune geometra and their response had been that if the comune wouldn't give us permission to alter our property, then go ahead and do it anyway! The advice was tempting, but we already knew the consequences if we were discovered, and so I asked around for third, fourth and fifth opinions from more neighbours. They were always the same. Everyone knew of people who had done what we wanted to do and got away with it. Some others said that they'd had similar works done and got away with it, because their properties had been passed onto family members and so when it came to selling it the abusivo label hadn't been put to the test.

Another year passed and pig-headed me, who has always found it hard to adhere to rules with which I don't agree, still wouldn't accept the geometra's decision, so I asked a builder friend from Moltrasio how much he estimated it would cost if he went ahead and did the work. He did give us an estimate, but he was reluctant to do the actual work, because if the geometra did find out that the work had been carried out, he would ask who did it, and because the project was abusivo he could fine the builder as well. We asked another builder we knew, but when we couldn't provide the vital document that granted permission he also backed away, for the same reason. We contacted a third builder who we didn't know, who agreed to do it. He was the most expensive of the three quotations we'd had, but that was his price for taking a risk and we knew if we didn't accept it, we would be unlikely to find anybody else willing to do the work. Our local electrician was the next to agree. Through another friend, we found somebody to fit the glazed doors and windows. He said his company would do it, but only if we agreed to pay the fine if we were found out. We said we would, without knowing how much it would be.

Three months later the work was finished, and the only way for the comune geometra to see what had been done would be for him to take a boat into the middle of the lake and look at the villa through his binoculars. If he did so, he would notice that the comparatively small area of glass fits in perfectly with the style of the villa and the other windows. He would also notice that the vast, ugly, four storied condominium two hundred metres up the road from us hadn't been finished and it never would be, because the owner was in jail for fraud. It is just one of dozens of properties around the lake and hundreds throughout Italy that remain unfinished because the banks have pulled the plug on loans. All these buildings are of course "creating volume".

Three years later the ruling, which allows for enormous condominiums to be constructed but not extensions to existing properties in Argegno was relaxed, but it only permits the addition of up to twenty cubic metres, subject to planning consent. This welcome transformation has allowed dozens of people like us, who have been waiting for years for the opportunity to add or alter their properties to do so, without having to look over their shoulders. We then immediately employed our geometra once again, to register the conversion. A year later it was recorded.

~~~

One of the principal reasons I wanted to open a studio was to display the watercolours and paintings of the lake and the local villages that I had in stock, to the public. Another reason was that I hoped it would mean my not having to work for the Como architect anymore. When we lived in Moltrasio my studio was in one of the main piazzas, which was an advantageous position for me to sell to tourists. Our villa in Argegno is away from the village centre, so to attract visitors I had the idea of making a small display of watercolours to put in the tourist information office, with some flyers and a map of where my studio was. I was hoping that tourists who might be looking to buy art would be interested enough to telephone for an appointment to view. It worked. The tourist information office was helpful and for a percentage of sales, they agreed to promote the display of paintings.

Among my first customers were the American golfer Jack Nicklaus and his wife. A few decades previously, Nicklaus had started a company that designs golf courses, and he had clients all around the world. He was in Italy looking for Italian bric-a-brac to decorate a new Italian-themed clubhouse in Florida that his company had built. He bought a large watercolour of the lake for it. Then, one afternoon I looked up from what I was painting as four giant American women walked into the studio and asked if they could have a wander around to look at some art. That is not me using non-PC language: they really were giants and they had been attending a convention of female giants in Milan. They had a spare day in their itinerary and so they had decided to spend it beside the lake. They all must have been at least seven feet tall and were very feminine. They all had a great sense of humour too. I said that seeing one female giant is a rarity but four together is astonishing. They said they were used to comments and being stared at. Although they didn't buy any art, they stayed chatting for at least half an hour. Besides them asking for my opinion on the best ristorante in the village, they also wanted to know if I knew of any male giants that lived locally, because they were looking for romance. I was tempted to recommend Fabio, but when they said they would need three giants, one each to keep them happy, I said I couldn't help them.

A couple of weeks later, an American couple from New York City arrived in my studio with one of my flyers in hand. Their names were Mike and Loren. They didn't buy anything but they stayed for an hour chatting and we got on really well. As they left, Mike said that if I was ever in NYC, his mother had an apartment in Manhattan on East 3rd Avenue that he'd rent to me for a good price.

Soon after they had gone, an air stewardess who worked for Delta Airlines bought a large Trompe l'Oeil chest of drawers that featured the Versace family's villa in Moltrasio. While I was packing it, she said if I ever wanted to go to the States she could fix me up with a "buddy pass". Each year she was allocated nine business class tickets for family and friends and as I'd just given her a large discount to tempt her to buy my wares she must have perceived me as a "buddy". I'd never been to the USA and always wanted to go. Then, six months after the flight offer, another New Yorker and his wife sought me out. They introduced themselves as Ed and Bev. Besides buying a watercolour, they asked if I would be interested in painting a mural in their stone farmhouse in Vermont, which they were in the process of refurbishing. Ed was an Italian American with thick, swept-back silver hair. He was almost a look-alike for the American chat show host Jay Leno, but without the jutting chin. He was the easy-going type, a big personality with a big, broad-shouldered body.

It seemed like providence - an offer of an apartment to rent in upper Manhattan, an open return flight to the US for three hundred dollars (a quarter of the business class price), and an offer of a mural commission seemed too good to turn down. So, one morning in late April of the following year, I dressed smartly in a black and maroon striped blazer, white shirt, a grey silk tie and tailored beige trousers, because I knew that a few hours later I would be sitting in the business class end of a Boeing 767, flying from Milan Malpensa to JFK airport in New York. What I didn't know was that the complimentary wine I would be drinking would be French. On board, I asked the stewardess for Italian wine, but they only served French. I hadn't tasted French wine for many years, because ninety-nine per cent of wine sold in Italy is Italian. The difference in flavour was instantly noticeable, and I wasn't keen on it. The same stewardess let me try four other wines they had on board, all of which had good brand names but I wasn't keen on them either. I'm not a connoisseur of wine, but give me Italian over French any day of the week.

I had arranged to meet the Delta stewardess at JFK an hour after landing. She would be changing flights at the same time and I wanted to present her with three antique prints of Lake Como as a gift for the favour she had done me. I then took a bus from the airport to the centre of Manhattan and then a taxi to the apartment on East 3rd Avenue, where I was met by a commissionaire, dressed in a maroon tail suit, top hat and yellow cotton gloves. He was standing underneath one of those striped canopies that extend from the main entrance and across the footpath to the curb edge that only the best apartment blocks have. As I went into the building it was clear to me that I'd landed on my feet, and on entering the fifth floor apartment I found I was sleeping in tip-top luxury for seventy-five bucks a night, the same price as a down-town one star hotel. And this very reasonable fee was only to pay the cleaning charge. Mike arrived a couple of hours later to see if everything was to my satisfaction and he told me that the apartment was opposite the one that Jacqueline Kennedy once owned. He offered to show me around New York, his home town. I was certainly staying in the right locality. Central Park was at the end of the block. Fifth Avenue, with the Guggenheim Museum to the south and the Metropolitan Museum of Art to the north was only a five-minute walk away.

I'd decided to spend a week sightseeing in Manhattan and to take in a few art exhibitions, especially at the Guggenheim and the Museum of Modern Art, before starting work on the mural in Vermont, because this might be a once in a lifetime opportunity to view the city. I had also taken my portfolio, with the intention of making some work contacts in the interior design business if the chance arose. To some extent I was successful, because while walking the city, if I saw a company that looked as if they could be useful, I'd call in. Amazingly, if the boss were in the building I would get to see him or her. Then, over coffee we would swap contact details and most of them said they would be in touch. If I tried cold calling in Italy or in the UK, which I had done in the past, I was usually shown the door before I'd said why I was there. I was so impressed and excited by the reaction of the interior designers I phoned Nicola to tell her that I might have to apply for a work permit when I got back so I could divide my time between Italy and the US, because compared to Europe it still appeared to be a land of opportunity. Her answer was 'go for it!'

It felt stimulating being in the States for the first time. New York City has a reputation for toughness, but after being welcomed by the yellow-gloved commissionaire, who said he'd spent most of his life standing on the street and had never felt unsafe, I felt reassured, especially when it was clear to see that the east side of Manhattan is primarily a wealthy neighbourhood. I had spent the early part of my life working and socialising in the centre of Liverpool, in the days when surviving there unscathed was an achievement. I was at the adventurous age and some of the places I used to end up, gaining life's experience, gave me the confidence to know that if I could survive in Liverpool then I could survive in most places. I'd also spent some years working and socialising in areas of London that were also considered to be dodgy, but I hadn't had any problems there either, because I always found that if I respected people and their terrain, confrontations were infrequent. Trouble can arrive when respect is forgotten and I never forget it, especially in a foreign country.

With eight million residents, New York City is the

largest city in the USA. When the Dutch settled there they called it New Amsterdam, but when the British arrived in the seventeenth century they renamed it New York. It was for sure a total contrast to Argegno with its six hundred inhabitants, and I was eager to start seeing it. The architecture was my main interest: this was what I'd always wanted to examine, especially my two favourites, the elegant Chrysler Building and the massive Empire State Building, which was regarded as the eighth wonder of the world when it was unveiled in 1931. My expectations were not let down - they are spellbinding in their magnificence, or to use a word that follows one and all around the city, "awesome".

To some people, the downtown Manhattan financial centre represents New York City. To others it represents the entire United States. I wasn't keen on the area. Although the buildings are impressive in both volume and construction, they don't have the character of say, the Lexington area, where narrow, four-storey brownstone town houses exist aplenty. I thought these icons, which make a satisfying sight, would have been demolished years ago to make space for steel, concrete and glass. To add to my delight, they still had external water towers on rooftops and ornate cast iron external fire escapes running up and down the sides.

The weather while I was there was hot and sunny, and the atmosphere was calm and quiet. I'd been expecting to be crushed by crowds on the subway trains but this never happened. In fact Manhattan has an easy-going, friendly spirit that made it the most relaxed city I've ever come across. I'd expected the noise from the large amount of traffic to be excessive, but what never ceased to amaze me was that there was hardly any noise. Taxis and buses drive around in a sedate manner and its as if they have very effective silencers in their exhaust systems: ten vehicles together in New York seemed to make as much noise as an individual vehicle would in any European city. And an efficient up-and-down intersection system reduces road congestion to a minimum. But the revelation - and a pleasing one - that struck me most was the large amount of space between the buildings. I never imagined there would be so much. After all, the reason for the skyscraper was to build more capacity on proportionately less ground space. Land in Manhattan Island was, and still is at a premium and I had imagined the buildings would be squashed together, preventing the sunlight from penetrating between them, but it was the opposite. According to Mike's mother, whom I met later, a lot of the original skyscrapers had been demolished and had been replaced by much taller, thinner skyscrapers, with the length of the shadow cast being taken into consideration before they were constructed. They are modern-day marvels of design and engineering that are still evolving and I felt privileged to be able to see and touch them.

I'd read that Manhattan was a series of individual villages. Such villages do exist in London, but not on the scale I came across in Manhattan. Although the residents of Manhattan feel they belong to a village, I'd call these districts small towns. Overall, I found it to be a friendly, well-presented and well-designed city, with wide tree-lined avenues and flowered boulevards that helped create good ventilation and I wouldn't have minded living there.

Another of the reasons I wanted to visit Manhattan was to find out "where it's at" in respect of the art world. If a place has a reputation for creativity I like to find where the influence is centred, because if it exists, it will say how progressive (or not) a place is. Art has a knock-on effect on a city's culture and if I cannot find it, I will ask bystanders, or people like Mike where this creativity is centred. He told me to go to Chelsea or Greenwich Village.

But although Manhattan has a reputation as a world leader in the arts, I looked hard but I couldn't find that creative heart. Art galleries are the place to begin such a search, especially the small private ones that feature contemporary artists, because they say immediately if the place has anything new to offer. But there wasn't an original spark in any of them. In fact, compared to London's private gallery scene, I'd seen it all before, and what's more, some years earlier. This was disappointing, but maybe the New York art scene will come again. Italy is in a similar situation to America, where its current art scene is uninspired. Italy's epoch for originality was five hundred years ago, when the Renaissance masters paraded their remarkable influence. Perhaps Manhattan's period of artistic originality was in the 1960s, when American pop art had an impact, or more likely, in the 1920s and 1930s, when the concept and design of its astonishing skyscrapers came to the fore. In the past, culture was centred in places like Florence, Rome and Paris, but perhaps for today the most creative art is digital and it is not represented geographically any longer. Maybe art has already been devoured by the global supermarket and there will never again be a definitive centre.

~~~

My last day in Manhattan was spent with Mike driving me to the areas of his city I hadn't been to. Naturally, "Little Italy", in Lower Manhattan was a must. On the way there he told me that hardly any Manhattanites own cars. Quite unlike any other segment of the American population, the locals either walk or use public transport because car insurance is ridiculously high, and monthly parking charges are more than the rent on a two-bedroom apartment. Hardly anybody owns a garage because so few of them exist and if one does come up for sale it will also cost more than the price of a two-bedroom apartment.

The neighbourhood of Little Italy was once - obviously - known for its large population of Italians. In the 1950s there were ten thousand, but as I soon discovered there are few if any Italians living there nowadays and today it's only nostalgia that brings the tourist there. We went to a bar and I heard some of the olive-skinned people who owned the place talking, but I couldn't recognise their language as Italian. I thought it might be a southern Italian dialect, but when I spoke to them in Italian, they didn't reply. We then went to a pizzeria for lunch that advertised itself as being Italian and when I tried to introduce some Italian into a conversation we were having with the staff, they looked at me as though I was soft in the head. According to Mike, Little Italy boasts Italian food stores, bars and restaurants, but they are not run by Italians. They are run by Romanians, who keep up the pretence of being Italian.

~~~

The day after I moved out of Mike's mother's apartment I met Ed's wife, Bev at her office in downtown Manhattan and she drove us to their impressive house in New Jersey to meet Ed. It was exactly a year since they visited my studio in Italy. I stayed there for two nights and on the Friday evening we drove the two hundred and fifty-mile, four-hour drive to their stone farmhouse near Vergennes in the State of Vermont, where I could begin painting the mural for them.

With a population of 2,700, Vergennes bills itself as America's smallest city. It is a peaceful, ordered and respectable town set towards the southern end of Lake Champlain, an old fashioned setting with a lot of beautiful wooden buildings, built and painted in typical American colonial style. There was an immediate feel of history about the place and I found out from an accountant friend of Ed's, who lived in one of the colonial buildings that Thomas MacDonough, who was the Commander of the American naval forces during the Second War of Independence, built a fleet of wooden ships in Vergennes.

This war, one theatre of which was Lake Champlain, lasted from 1812 to 1815. The battle that took place on Lake Champlain was significant, because the occupying British navy suffered a heavy defeat that hastened the end of the war, with the Treaty of Ghent being signed by the English Prince Regent soon after it was over.

Ed was the owner of a large trucking business based in New Jersey that transported paper for printing purposes all over the States. He was semi-retired, so all he had to do was keep in touch with the running of the business while his partners did the work. I wanted to get on with painting but as he had all day and every day to himself he seemed keen that I should be his golf partner and general playmate for a few weeks. I had to keep reminding him that I wasn't on holiday and we must get down to talking about a design for his mural.

Ed was so Italian in character and temperament that at times when I was talking to him I forgot I was in the USA and not in Italy. However, he couldn't speak a word of Italian – he always pronounced the word "eye-talian". He was a fun guy with a big heart who liked to celebrate the enjoyable things in life as all Italians do and I liked him a lot. He called me his buddy. He'd say to his wife, 'me and my buddy are going to buy some paint for the mural.' This happened to be true on one occasion when he persuaded me to accompany him, but it wasn't on two others. Buying paint was an excuse for him to get out of the house so he could stop off at his favourite diner for a late, second breakfast. When he introduced me to the diner he said, 'whatever you do, don't tell Bev where we've been or what I ate or she'll kill me.'

At first I was pleased, because another thing I'd always wanted to do while I was in America was visit a diner. I'd seen the Hollywood films with people sitting at long counters, tucking into what looked like pleasing home style cooking. I was fascinated by Edward Hopper's painting called "The Diner", and so in some ways I was a bad influence for Ed, because I didn't say no when he suggested visiting one on the way to the centre of Vergennes for an unnecessary breakfast.

The American institution known as the Diner predates McDonald's by decades. Nothing typifies 1950s America quite like it, transporting people back to the days of jukeboxes, poodle skirts and open top Cadillacs. Diners serve American food with an emphasis on fried or griddled breakfast items. There are hamburgers - naturally; several ways of cooking eggs - scrambled, over easy or sunny side up (I always wanted to say to a diner waitress 'give me my eggs sunny-side-up!') French fries, waffles, pancakes, sausages, hash browns, ham and French toast. Many diners serve these 'breakfast foods' any time of the day and evening.

A neon sign over the door of this one said, "Welcome to our 24 hour a day Diner". High up behind the counter was the menu, written in big, bold, red letters on a large white board. Although it was written in English, I didn't understand what any of it meant. Apart from the double and triple burgers that were also advertised, none of the items listed had explanations as to what they were. Both Ed and the woman who was doing the cooking looked uninterested when I asked them to translate the names into something I could recognise, but between them they attempted to coach me. These exotic-sounding dishes were:

Daddy's Home: three eggs and toast, with a choice of bacon, ham, sausage, home fries, two pancakes, slice of French toast.

Break it to Me Gently: omelette with five types of cheese - cheddar, provolone, Swiss, pepper jack; onions, green peppers, mushrooms, hot peppers and bacon.

South of the Border: omelette with cheddar cheese, salsa and deep fried jalapeño peppers, served with home fries, bacon, ham or sausage.

Teardrops on my Pillow: Pierogi (Polish) style

dumplings stuffed with garlic mashed potatoes and onions, American cheese with home fries and a choice of bacon, ham, sausages or toast.

Jailhouse Rock: a breakfast sandwich of home-style bread grilled to perfection, with two eggs, cheese and a choice of bacon, ham or sausages and served with home fries.

Three Coins in the Fountain: a stack of fluffy homemade buttermilk pancakes, served with butter and maple syrup.

Texas Home Gal: two slices of French bread, two jumbo sausages and two fried eggs, served with maple syrup.

Pigs in a Blanket: Two jumbo sausages rolled in pancakes with maple syrup

Carmen Miranda: Bananas Foster (French toast with bananas and pecans) with caramelised brown sugar sauce.

The Brando: turkey melt with American cheese, lettuce and tomato.

Greased Lightning: grilled ham with cheese of your choice.

Bye-bye Birdie: two slices of bread with one egg nestled in the centre of each slice, grilled to perfection, served with a choice of bacon, hash browns, home fries or sausages.

I wasn't much the wiser after they'd described what each one was, but I'd got them all mixed up and was in a mild flap. Ed and the waitress were waiting for me to order and it was obvious the proprietress had a short fuse, or thought I was either stupid or I was taking a rise out of her, because she'd placed her hands on her hips. This to me is always a sign that a woman's patience is wearing thin. So, I apologised for my ignorance and asked if I could possibly have something that wasn't too heavy.

'Dig that accent!' she said.

'He's an Englishman who speaks eye-talian,' Ed said. And to help me out of my predicament, added, 'Give him a Texas!'

I watched the woman whisk two eggs in a bowl and then dip two slices of white sliced bread in it until they were soggy. Then she slapped them on the griddle for a few seconds until they had crisped up a bit, then flipped them over. She then took two jumbo sausages out of a pan of lukewarm water and placed them on the bread. She quickly fried two eggs sunny-side-up (without me getting the opportunity to ask for them that way), balanced them neatly on top of the sausages and poured maple syrup - a lot of maple syrup - over all of it. Then she took a transparent plastic one-pint beaker and filled it to the brim with flat, machine coke that I hadn't asked for but Ed had. I ate it, and drank some of the coke, but I have to say it I didn't enjoy it. I'd been alarmed by the way the cook mixed savoury food with sweet. But as we were very near to Canada, which is the home of maple syrup, so I supposed it was a regular local dish. But then why was it called a "Texas"?

And it was a case of quantity without quality. The ingredients were second rate and, I guessed cheap. They would have to have been to keep the prices low. There was no flavour to the Texas except grease and sugary syrup. Nor was it real maple syrup, but pancake syrup, because real maple syrup is very expensive. After the first diner visit we left with a bag of bagels because I'd never eaten those either. I'd also seen them being eaten in films, so Ed bought them for me as a treat. They were saturated in garlic, and although I am a big garlic fan I found them as awful as the food the diner had dished up.

What Ed saw in the place, I don't know. No wonder his wife was anti-diner. This wasn't the only time we went to Ed's favourite Diner during the time I worked for him, but I refrained from eating and stuck to the watery coffee. I'd been spoilt by living in Italy. There is no comparison whatsoever between the quality of food and cooking in a real Italian trattoria against that of a diner. I have to say that it was in Manhattan that, for the first time in my life I sent a meal back because it was so awful. I believe they just miss it in the States when it comes to food. In my experience, the only way to eat well there it seems is to pay over the top or eat at home.

Ed and Bev had to return to their home in New Jersey early every Monday because Bev had to go to work, but the day before they went, Ed would take me food and beer shopping to the nearest supermarket so I could stock up for my working week while they were away. From then until they returned, I was left in charge of their stone house. Ed kept repeating the expression, 'stone house' as if it was some big deal. I guess it was because he said it could never be knocked down. It was part of a region of farms and homesteads, set in hundreds of acres of undulating, open farmland, with tall silos and red barns, surrounded by hills and snow-capped mountains in the far distance. Ed and Bev's stone house was five miles out of Vergennes town and as we drove to and from it I couldn't help singing the words of the Great American Songbook classic, "Moonlight in Vermont", which describes the telegraph cables running down the highway and the ski trails that run down the mountainsides.

It only took me an hour to design Ed and Bev's mural. They wanted me to paint the mural in their sunroom. It was on a side of the house that didn't have much of a view, so they decided they wanted a landscape on the wall. The Vermont countryside is picturesque, with lots of grazing cattle, so I took the view from the front of the house and brought it into the sunroom, adding their red barn and silo to the composition. To give it a Trompe l'Oeil touch, I painted the white rails that border each farm as the foreground feature, so the viewer had the impression they were looking out from a corral.

Thanks to Ed's diversions, the mural hadn't been progressing as well as it should have been, so I made sure I knuckled down during the weekdays, extending the working day to around twelve hours, because Ed and Bev would be back the following Friday evening. Ed's weekend calendar would be all-encompassing and he would want me to come out to play, so I would have to seal the lids on the colours for a couple of days to stop them drying out.

~~~

One Saturday morning Ed looked a bit meditative and when Bev wasn't around he told me it was her fiftieth birthday soon and did I have any ideas about what he should buy her. I suggested buying her a bunch of flowers.

He replied, 'I was thinking of something more like a car.'

So, off we went in his un-restored, pea-green 1946 Chevrolet stepside pick-up truck to view a 1958 Lancia Aurelia Spider, a two-seater Italian sports car he'd seen advertised for sale in a car magazine. He bought it for her, and the weekend after, he held a Sunday lunchtime birthday party for Bev at their house. It was full of his eye-talian American friends, who all had a great time. Curiously, although they looked exactly like the Italians I had lived amongst for the previous two decades, none of them spoke a word of Italian. Ed introduced me as an Englishman who speaks eye-talian and he wanted me to give them a demonstration of my linguistic skills.

He was in a buying mood and the next day he took me to a showroom to view a four-berth sea-going houseboat he was considering buying that would take them to Florida each winter. And after that he took me to a car repair garage that contained eleven impressive Ferraris, but it wasn't to buy one. It was to meet the guy that ran it, another eye-talian American who imported second hand and vintage Ferraris that he and his staff refurbished and sometimes rebuilt for the American market. Once again Ed said, 'Say something to him in eye-talian!' So I did, but the Ferrari dealer didn't understand a word of it.

One of the restored Ferraris was bound for Brescia in

northern Italy in a week's time, where the garage owner planned to race it in the modern recreation of the historic Mille Miglia road race. Unfortunately, we heard that Ed's friend had to drop out after only two days of racing as something broke in the gearbox and it was too long a job to fix.

~~~

When the mural was finished Bev introduced me to Suzy, an interior designer and close friend of hers who was working on their house and who said she wanted some artwork in her pantry. She came up with an idea to paint extinct birds on several door panels leading to the kitchen, and so I swapped homes for two weeks to create Suzy's image. Here I experienced another homely, American-style welcome, with Suzy's husband Doug taking me for a spin in his speedboat on Lake Champlain. I thought Lake Como was big until I saw Lake Champlain. It was so big it was like being at sea and there were waves big enough to rock the boat. Half an hour out of the Vergennes dock, the land on the opposite bank looked a long way off. They took me to a restaurant one evening where I shook the hand of Johannes von Trapp, who was sitting at a nearby table. He is a surviving member of the original von Trapp singing family, on whose life the film The Sound of Music was based. When the family left Austria in the early 1940s they emigrated to Stowe in Vermont.

In any case, moving house and working for Suzy didn't mean I'd seen the last of Ed. He'd decided to spend a week without his wife at their Vergennes home and he came to visit me on most days to see how I was progressing with Suzy's panels, or that's what he said, but it was really to enquire if I was bored with painting, because if I was, he could arrange for us to go out and play some. May 27th was Vergennes Memorial Day. It was a Sunday when Ed and Bev took me with them to watch hundreds of people taking part in a one mile parade of cheerleaders, colourful period costumes, floats, parade horses, vintage vehicles, veteran groups and boy and girl scouts. Accompanied by more, very acceptable homemade food and drink.

The day Suzy's pantry door panels were finished I telephoned Ed to come and pick me up to take me back to his place for a day or two. Bev was back in Manhattan working at her office and so the intention was that Ed and I would play some, but he wasn't in form. He suffered from recurring kidney stones and he was in pain. The following morning we left very early with me driving his Mercedes to his hospital in New Jersey, were we met Bev in the lobby. It was an untimely goodbye and it was said in haste as a couple of nurses led him into surgery. Bev then drove me to the nearest railway station and put me on a train heading for Hoboken, New Jersey.

After two months in America, it was time to go home. Most probably I could have stayed and worked in the country for a lot longer, because after the Vermont adventure I went back to Manhattan for a further five days, mainly to fulfil some appointments I'd made with some interior design companies based in the D & D (Decoration and Design) Building on 3rd Avenue, close to Bloomingdale's. One of them had ideas for me to paint a couple of murals for a Connecticut client, starting more or less immediately, but they would have been large projects and I just didn't have the time or the required documentation to take on large, commercial work.

I also met my daughter and her partner outside the Museum of Modern Art. They live in Wales and I hadn't seen them for three years. They happened to be holidaying in Boston, which I didn't know and they didn't know I was working in the States, but when we found out they decided to stop off for a couple of days so we could meet up and "play some", as Ed would say, before they flew home. And speaking of Ed, he had successful laser surgery to break up his kidney stones and he was back home in no time. He and Bev have been over to see us since.

13 Young at Heart

It took me two days to recover and re-acclimatise to Argegno's capricious community after two months in the USA. I'd missed Nicola, I'd missed our cats and I'd missed our home. I'd also missed the village, so later that week I wandered down to the piazza to buy some vegetables from the market. I was also interested to see how my aged "eye-talian buddies" were faring around the fountain, because I wanted to tell them about my American experience. Whether they would be interested in listening would be debatable, but I was going to have a go anyway, to try and bring something a bit different to the morning's discussion. But when I got there nobody was there. It was eleven in the morning and in mid July that meant the temperature was in the 30s. So where were they? There was no sign of anyone, so I headed in the direction of the Bar Onda, which, if the weather were doubtful would be their alternative venue. They weren't in there either so I asked the barman if he knew where they all were? He said that he hadn't seen them recently, but if they weren't in the piazza, then I should look in the Bar Ponte.

'Che strano (how strange)!' I thought. I backtracked across the main piazza and past the fountain, taking a right turn towards the Bar Ponte. Sure enough, when I looked through the window, there they were - eight of the terrible ten, huddled around a green baize card table. I was greeted well by half of them, but the other four looked a bit dismayed, until I reminded them of where I'd been. One of them even said he thought I'd emigrated and he was surprised I'd returned.

I asked them why they were all inside on such a blissfully warm day, but there was a pause before a few sneaky grins spread across some of their faces. A couple of them took deep breaths, blew them out noisily, sighed and rolled their eyes. Then Alessandro stood up, beckoned me to put my head closer to his and cupped his hands around my ear. In a forceful whisper he said, 'look at the barmaid. That's why!' He made a space for me to sit down at the table and mouthed, 'turn around now, she's behind the bar!'

Surreptitiously I turned to look, to see the only female in the place. She was tall, young and well proportioned, with blonde hair cut in a striking way, turquoise eyes and a beautiful face. And she was definitely not Italian. It was obvious from then on why the old boys had changed their venue, because without a shadow of a doubt she was a stunner. I couldn't help wondering why she had chosen to work behind an unfashionable village bar when she could have been on a catwalk in Milan.

To give me the opportunity to see the rest of her, Alessandro waved an empty Pinot Grigio bottle above our heads to gain her attention and flashed his whitened teeth at her. Putting on his over-friendly boyish charm, he asked her to replace it with a full one saying, 'è Paul a comprare (it's Paul's turn to buy)!' His intention was to get her to walk across the open bar floor so I could judge her for myself. For sure she had what it takes.

When she had taken the empty bottle and was out of

earshot, I asked the old boys who she was, and where she was from. It turned out that a month previously the bar owner had advertised for a new barmaid. When this girl answered, he took her on and within the first week his business doubled as word spread about her. She had been a student and she had a degree but the old boys didn't know in what. They did know she was Ukrainian and she couldn't find work in her own country, so she applied for a visa to enter Italy and she was staying with her aunt in Tremezzo. She hadn't got a boyfriend but they reckoned she soon would have, because in the evenings the bar was full of young guys, competing with each other to take her home on the back of their scooters. Apart from that, the old boys didn't know much else about her, except her name was Katrina, that she was aged twenty-two and they couldn't resist her. 'That's all any man needs to know!' Enzo said.

Katrina had certainly got the old boys at it and I wasn't altogether sure that her being there during their daily aperitivi hour before they went home for their lunches was good for their indifferent health. Every time they looked up from their pretext of a card game she was there to rekindle their covetous hankerings. Every time she moved a muscle, time froze momentarily. This natural blonde held them enraptured to the point of embarrassment. Their eyeballs boggled, and every time she came near to the table their tongues fell out of the corner of their mouths. As for those with a devious mind, it was an opportunity to sneak a glance at the hand of cards of the person they were sitting beside. Under his breath, Enrico said she was the most gorgeous thing he'd ever seen. And under *his* breath, Pino said she was driving him insane. Mario said he couldn't sleep at night thinking about her. Bruno said that since she'd arrived on the scene, the pains in his joints had disappeared. Alessandro said he was sure she was in love with him. 'Poor girl,' I said. 'She must wonder what has hit her.'

Alessandro introduced me to her, making sure she knew I was English, and out of politeness she smiled a huge smile, flushed slightly, held her hand out and then said, 'ello, I am very pleased to meet you, yes?'

Not only was she beautiful, she seemed nice as well and I thought it was no wonder they had taken to her. There was, however, rivalry for her attentions from another set of old boys, because on the opposite side of the room there were a couple of tables reserved for the card-playing regulars of the Bar Ponte. They were well aware why the lot who used to keep the seat around the fountain warm were gate-crashing their territory and they would grimace every time Katrina busied herself around our table and not theirs. But they were only friendly grimaces, accompanied by a protective smugness that implied she was their property. They were prepared to share her with us, as long as we remembered whom she belonged to.

The bar was filling up as lunchtime got nearer, with the local workers popping in for a quick aperitivo and a cigarette before they had to shoot off to their homes to eat, so Katrina was busy. It was also time for the old boys to leave for their homes. The water for the pasta would be nearing boiling point, giving them eleven minutes to get home from the time the spaghetti is put into the pan for it to be served al dente.

There are eight bars in Argegno and each has its own regulars. They all know each other and they also know the regulars who frequent the other bars. Also, the bar owners know their customers and they know the other bar owners as well as they know their own brothers. During the day they will regularly pop into a neighbour's bar for a drink and a chat. Now that Katrina was on the scene, the other bar owners realised that to compete with the Bar Ponte's sudden upturn in business they had better employ a good-looking barmaid, especially at night-time when the youth is out and about. Bar Ponte had taken on the atmosphere of a trendy 'night', while the other bars were beginning to find it wasn't worth staying open.

However, and perhaps fortuitously the heart rate of the ageing late morning aperitivi male population was finally restored to normal two weeks later, when Katrina's hours where changed to evenings. The old boys don't go out in the evenings, preferring to watch football, basketball or cycling on Sky Italia and then go to bed early. Also, the other bar owners had also employed attractive young barmaids, so custom was evenly spread once more. So, once out of sight, Katrina dropped off the old boys' radar and as there was nothing else to look at during the morning session, they drifted back to fountain. God works in mysterious ways and he must have had a relapse when he installed Katrina in Argegno, but thankfully he had come to his senses when he realised what he had done, and had put the notion in Katrina's employer's head to change her shift before it all became too silly.

~~~

The working day of Italian bar owners and their staff is a long one. They will open at six in the morning to serve people on their way to work in desperate need of a strong espresso with their cigarette. If the twice-weekly draw for the Super Enlotto (lottery) is due, their customers will want to buy tickets. Around nine-thirty there will be an hour's lull when they wash the crockery and tidy the bar. Then the office workers will pop in for a quick mid-morning caffè, followed an hour later by the local old boys for their aperitivi. This will last until the workers start arriving for their lunchtime drinks and a cooked snack. After lunch there will be a change of staff, the chance to wash up again and a lull until siesta time is over. Then the old men return for a caffè or a glass of wine. After they've gone, the staff will prepare for the early evening rush, when the workers arrive to enjoy happy hour. This will finish around seven, followed by another lull and a further change of staff, who will prepare for the late evening crowd. In Italy a lot of people eat their main meal at home and then around eight-thirty, they go to a bar for a caffè and a dessert and possibly a drink. This is also cocktail time, when the young people arrive. In summer, some tourist bars offer live music and they will remain open until the last customer leaves.

Before Katrina had her working hours altered, I had the chance to catch up on the gossip I'd missed out on whilst I'd been in the States. At one of our mid-morning sessions, Katrina's stimulating presence must have got Luigi motivated, because he began filling me in about something that should have remained private. Luigi is seventy-six and looks good for his age, although he dyes his hair. If he had told me when I first met him he was fifty-six and not seventy-six I would have believed him. Thinking about it, it's only he and Vittorio who aren't always reminding us of how ill they are. For thirty-five years, Luigi was a top chef in some of Como's better restaurants, but he has struggled to come to terms with retirement. He cannot sit still for long. He gesticulates and stands up a lot, especially when he is having his say, and it will take one of us to remind him that he is standing and another one to persuade him to sit down again. His temperament is classically Italian; he lives off his nerves. Still, it must be good for him, because it keeps him slim and young looking.

I hadn't seen him for nearly a year, but most of the old boys said this was because he had been at the reunions on the days that I hadn't and vice versa. He's like me, I think, enjoying a reunion now and again rather than all the time. On this particular occasion he arrived wearing an immaculate new cream cotton chino suit with a red rose in the buttonhole. Mario asked him if he'd bought it for his wedding. 'No,' Luigi replied. 'Just the opposite!' Apparently he'd just been to see his lawyer to discuss intricacies regarding his divorce and he thought he had better look smart for the occasion.

'Divorce?' I asked. 'What divorce?'

Luigi's life-changing revelation was that while I'd been away, he'd proposed marriage to a much younger woman. I think I said, 'Jesu Cristo!'

Mario said that it wasn't Katrina, if that was what I was thinking. It was with somebody else's wife. 'Oh,' I muttered. 'That's alright, then.'

It transpired that Luigi wanted a change, and his face was certainly flushed in anticipation as he expanded on what he'd started. 'There is no law of nature saying you have to love the woman you're married to,' he said.

I then discovered, courtesy of some of the others that the lady in his life (who he had been having an affair with for the past fifteen years), was only fifty-two years old. Questioning his impression that he thought he was immortal, I asked him what future he saw with a woman twenty-four years his junior. He said he believed he was good for years to come. But was this woman as mad as he was? If she was, then what hope was there for rationality?

'There is no virtue without immorality,' Luigi pronounced, and then he suddenly sat down and held his index finger against his shut lips. The golden vision that is Katrina had arrived and she leant over our table to remove our dirty glasses and wipe the table. Luigi didn't want her to hear, as if it were likely that she could make sense out of what I could not.

In Italy a conversation may be conducted using dozens of hand gestures, and it is wise to learn at least the important ones, otherwise what someone might say may be misunderstood. Behind Luigi's back, Mario pressed his two index fingers side by side. This implies that two people are getting along and possibly having sexual relations. Then in complete contradiction (and this was the confusing part), he pressed the tips of the same fingers against each other, suggesting that two people are not getting on, but are probably still having sexual relations.

Alessandro, who happened to be standing behind where Luigi was now sitting, made the sign of the cross over the top of Luigi's head, indicating that there was no hope for him, at the same time looking up to the ceiling and rolling his eyes. He then put his hands together as if he were praying to God to make this man sane again. Then Luigi turned around and when he saw what Alessandro was doing I thought he was going to explode for a moment, but instead he slid his chair back, knelt on one knee, kissed the back of Alessandro's hand and asked him for his blessing. 'The flesh is stronger than the scandal it will cause,' he said. 'But I am prepared to duel for her.'

When Katrina had gone back to the bar, Luigi continued with his story. He was in despair, because he only met with the woman he said he wanted to spend the rest of his life with when he could get her husband out of the way. To make matters worse, he'd been to see the priest to ask for his advice on how to go about marriage after adultery. Further, his intended's husband had only just been informed about what had been going on for the past fifteen years and rather than being possessive and furious about the scenario it emerged he could be "bought". It seemed he would be prepared to bow out gracefully and had agreed to a divorce, if a price he had in his mind for his wife's hand was met. The woman's husband had a taste for cognac, and Luigi had the wherewithal to soak him in it until he was ready to combust. It could yet end in bitter tears, especially as he, Luigi wanted God to sanction sex with another man's wife. 'The flesh of her flesh,' he said, 'is the dearest of all flesh.'

I said, 'You're a poet and you don't know it.'

Lorenzo said it was the Pinot Grigio talking.

Clearly, Luigi was making a fool of himself. It was as if he had been booked as the bar room entertainer. He seemed unable to look at himself objectively and realise his friends were laughing at his torment. They were encouraging him to appear more foolish by the moment, and he kept on providing them with more material. Luigi's pride was costing him a lot, because it was making him behave out of keeping. Why the man couldn't be content to stay in his *orto* (his allotment) and tend his tomatoes like any other seventy-six-year-old does, was baffling.

Luigi then asked me if I knew who it was he was hooked on.

'Of course I don't.' I replied.

'It's the former garage mechanic's wife,' Vittorio said.

It's no secret that Italian men of the old school consider themselves as romantics. They can be extremely expressive when it comes to emotions, and their women should be prepared for a lot of kissing and fondling. In their outgoing way they will tell a woman they hardly know, but have a fancy for, that until she has made love to him she doesn't know what love is. They will tell her they are committed to pleasing her and are attuned to all her needs and desires. 'Throw your inhibitions out of the door,' they will tell her, 'and get ready for the time of your life in the bedroom.'

The Italian male is prone to believe that once a woman has slept with him she is his forever, even if they are no longer in a relationship. He is extremely possessive and gets jealous if the woman he regards as his property should glance at another man in the wrong way.

Luigi then told me that forty-seven years ago, only five years after he and his wife had married, she'd had an affair. He'd only just found out about it, and it was plain that his pride had been woefully injured. For around the tenth time that morning he rose from his chair, clearing his throat as he did so, as if he was about to make a speech. Then, in a rather high pitched whine, rather than his normal voice he announced, 'it has to be stated that the relationship I had with my wife for fifty-two years was the most beautiful there has ever been, but now it has all vanished. When we were in love I used to take her on days out in my car. I used to write her poetry and I sang love songs to her. I bought her flowers and jewellery. I cooked special meals for her and bought her the best wines in Lombardia. I scratched her back for her and I massaged her feet. I fed her cat and I fixed the house and only four weeks ago I found out that all the time I was doing those things, she was doing it with another man as well as with me. Okay, he has been dead for the past twenty years, otherwise I would have killed him the minute I found his love letters.'

'What love letters?' I asked.

Luigi asked his friend Vittorio to continue telling me the rest of story. He said he couldn't tell it again because it made him so distraught that it felt like it was cutting him in half. While Luigi wiped his tearful eyes and the others embraced him as if they were comforting a close friend at a funeral, Katrina was asked to deliver him a stiff restorative as quickly as she could, to help his fragile disposition.

Vittorio's testimony was a lot more controlled and subdued than Luigi's had been, which was a relief. Apparently, Luigi had been clearing out some wardrobes when he came across a box with a pile of letters in it that had been sent to his wife over a period of three years. On reading some of them, he discovered that forty-seven years before, his wife had been having an affair. She had forgotten she had hidden the letters, and when Luigi confronted her, all was laid bare about the affair, and it was clear from the content of the letters that it had been very passionate. Not only that, but during those three years a daughter had been born and although his wife had insisted the baby was his, he was uncertain about this. The daughter, now aged forty-five had lived at home until she was twenty-five, then emigrated to Australia to marry. Luigi hadn't yet told her about the recent revelation, because he said he didn't know how to go about informing her that he might not be her father. I didn't make comment, because it wasn't anything to do with me, but I got the impression that his daughter was about the only person that didn't know she might be illegitimate, because everybody else in the bar, and possibly the whole village knew, because he'd been telling them all what a Jezebel his wife was.

Luigi started his affair with the former garage mechanic's wife fifteen years after his wife had been having her affair. So, on the same day he found the letters in the wardrobe, he went to see the former garage mechanic's wife to tell her what his wife had been doing with the guy who wrote the explicit letters and whilst he was there he told her (the former garage mechanic's wife), that she had always been his true love, and spontaneously proposed to her, pending his divorce from his current wife and her divorce from her husband. A few days later, it transpired that a price of €8,000 had been agreed for the former garage mechanic's wife hand in marriage, which he had already transferred into the former garage mechanic's bank account. He had also agreed to pay the divorce costs for both parties.

The rest of the old boys would wait to see how Luigi's injured pride would be when all the proceedings were completed, but the odds were not in favour of things working out the way he had planned. As soon as he walked out on his wife, Luigi rented a rather shabby bedsit next to the Bar Onda, at the back of the village in a spot without sunlight or a view of the lake. But we all believed it was more than likely that the former garage mechanic's wife would not leave her stylish house overlooking the lake to move into the bedsit, and that Luigi would never see his money again.

14 Traditional Values

When we arrived in Italy we came with the enthusiasm and determination necessary to make a move abroad a success. Italy is a magnificent and majestic country and although comparatively small, it has a large number of diverse cultures. We settled in an ancient village with a society that has, by and large remained unchanged for centuries. We didn't have to grow to love Italy; it implanted itself on us the minute we crossed the tarmac at Malpensa airport on April 9 1991 and our enthusiasm for Italian village life hasn't diminished to this day. I don't imagine it ever will.

Before we moved to Italy I had visited the country on three occasions as a tourist, and always went to the cities. But the way of life in the cities is entirely different from that of the villages, and as we settled we found we had entered what seemed like a time warp. Italy reminded me of life back in England when I was around seven years old. The television programmes were presented in an old fashioned way and popular music on the radio was out of date. The rolling stock of the national rail network dated from the nineteen sixties. Food shopping was how I remember it when I was only as high as the counter. At the village grocery store everything was individually wrapped in sheets of white or greaseproof paper and you could buy a single free-range egg the grocer would wrap in half a sheet of newspaper, instead of having to buy a pack of six in a plastic container. At the cold meat counter a shop assistant hand-sliced our order, then decided what size of brass weight to use to balance the scales.

On the opposite side of the street, Angelo the greengrocer would carefully pack our basket for us or deliver it on foot, proud of the freshness of his home grown produce. The butcher assured us that all his meat and poultry was from his own farm and didn't contain hormones. Going to the barber was how it was when my mother used to escort me. The post office still used rubber stamps and duplicated everything with carbon paper. We even had to lick our own stamps. At the bank, standing orders and direct debits didn't exist. We had to pay bills in cash or by cheque.

Of the other things I'd forgotten that Italian village life reawakened was not everybody had mains gas and for the residents that had bottled gas a delivery van would visit the village we lived in every Wednesday morning, when householders would swap their empty propane bottles for full ones. The house we rented in Moltrasio had both mains gas and electricity, but some of our neighbours didn't and they also used oil lamps for lighting, a log fire for heating and an iron, wood fired range for cooking and boiling water. I remember my aunt Winifred in Formby lived like that back in the mid 1950s. All the villages had (and still have) a free public washhouse for laundry. Bars of soap are provided by the Comune and some of the older women to this day use the large sinks, sharing the wringing out of heavier articles with a willing relative or friend.

The centre of Argegno village has remained much the same for the past nine hundred years and this has been dictated by the remains of what was a massive, twelfth century stone fort. Parts of the fort still dominate the village centre, even though over the centuries it has been reduced in size. What remains has gradually been converted into living accommodation and the part that fronts the main piazza is now the Ristorante Barchetta.

Italian culture is distinctive; at once recognisable, defined by customs and traditions, but also the diverse creative pursuits of each region. Because of Italy's tumultuous history and relatively recent unification, there is less emotional connection to the concept of being 'Italian' and answering to a central government in Rome, and more identification with a home town or region. Italians also form bonds with their neighbours and friends and refer to those from the same area or region as a *paisano*. As well as economic and political factors, creative events, festivals and celebrations also make up Italian culture. And although it has sometimes been portrayed in a less than positive light in many films, especially in stories about the Mafia, the innate friendliness of the people, their love of debate, their appreciation of the moment, their love of food, quality wines, good company and their struggle for excellence in whatever they do are why visitors enjoy Italy.

And there are unique events in towns and villages around the country. Every New Year's Day, the residents of Argegno hold a *Presepe Vivente*, a living Nativity. Many Italian villages, including our former home, Moltrasio hold presepe, which are nativity displays featuring life-size figures, but this one is unique, because it features real people and animals to depict scenes from the Nativity. The Presepe Vivente has been around for a long time but in the last decade it has become an important fixture on the village calendar. An ever-growing number of visitors from the Como province and beyond come to watch, so from what was originally a local event has grown into national even international spectacle. When Nicola and I first saw the Presepe Vivente in 2004 there were around a thousand people in attendance. The 2017 it drew over three thousand people. The costumes, props, and the artistic direction in general have improved from good to outstanding; so much so that the standard of the skill, detail and the effort are at professional level. And all this for an event that lasts for just two hours.

Days before the event, a local group, The Friends of Argegno decorate the streets with branches of pine and laurel and twenty or so *artigiani* (tradesmen) erect the scenery and build pounds and stables for the animals, making the already medieval village look positively ancient. Weeks of work will have gone into making the scenery and costumes that will decorate the piazzas, lanes, tracks, alcoves and the doorways; even the local men who will be taking part will have grown full beards.

Then, on the night before the event, the artigiani work to erect the scenery. When the other villagers wake up they find, right outside their front door either a recreation of Bethlehem as it was 2000 years ago, the inside of King Herod's Palace or, opposite their kitchen window a huge stone that has been rolled to one side to reveal Christ's sepulchre. And if the unsuspecting should venture out, they could bump into Saint Peter with a gang of fishermen in tow, on their way to cast their nets into the river Telo. They will certainly see a huge entourage of visitors arriving in Argegno to view the event as they pass over the Roman footbridge to stand outside the starting point of the procession, the Church of the Holy Trinity, where a 3 o'clock mass will be held before the participants set off.

The sun will be bright, but not warm. Set low in the sky, it will cast long shadows, reminding all who have gathered that they have just entered the first month of a New Year. Then, when all is ready the gathering will follow three elaborately clothed, gift-bearing Magi on horseback along the twists and turns of fifteenth century mule paths. The visitors are led back to the Roman Bridge, from where they will climb to the oldest part of the village, passing what were once the houses of the contadini - the poor people who used to work the mountain homesteads and pastoral farms or fish the vast lake. These poor people were often scorned by townsfolk as ignorant peasants. But not on this day. The townspeople will be on their best behaviour, some of them wishing they could swap places with the contadini instead of living in overcrowded suburbs. Contadini families themselves left their ancient villages to follow fortune and some, if they could, would welcome a return to how life was led in their old communities.

The people following the procession will have been given a written guide, telling them about the history of each particular biblical scene. In at least thirty five biblical representations, approximately eighty Argegnini, willing to confront whatever weather January throws at them will be in place, standing or sitting, silent and motionless, as if in a painting, (and hoping the animals will stay still) as the visitors pass by, eager to see how accurately the Bible stories have been interpreted. Each year the final stage is different, 2015's being a recreation of Leonardo di Vinci's *L'ultimo Cena* (The Last Supper), a long trestle table, covered with a white tablecloth with Jesus in the centre and his apostles on either side.

When the locals wake up the following morning it would be as if the presepe had happened in a dream, as any sign of it will have disappeared and everything will have been put back to normal. Even the huge amount of clearing up will have been done to a professional standard. All the animals, including two cows, several sheep, half a dozen mules and the same amount of donkeys, plus ducks, dogs, chickens, a dove, three horses and a herd of goats will have been loaded into trucks or in horse boxes and returned to the people who kindly lent them for this very special and well appreciated occasion.

Modernism is creeping up on the lakeside communities, but there is at least one person, who lives in the village of Laglio, six kilometres south of Argegno who is fighting to stem the tide. He is Achille the barber, a fit, lively and very friendly eighty-two-year-old. Every time I visit Achille I am transported back to the carefree days of my childhood when my mother used to take me, because his shop and the way he goes about his work hasn't changed for over half a century. What will happen on the day he decides to hang up his scissors for good doesn't bear thinking about, because it is unlikely anyone younger will take over his business and the only alternative for us men will be to go to a unisex hairdresser in a vast shopping mall twenty-five kilometres away; the kind of shop where you have to make an appointment. A female junior washes your hair and a slightly older one cuts it and all for an astronomical price. I'm sure that the occasional tourist who passes Achille's shop pretends he can do with a haircut, so that for a few minutes he can be transported back in time. A couple of years ago I asked Achille if he had ever estimated the number of heads he had cut since he started work before and through the war years, when he was employed as a barber in the army. He hadn't done so, so one day when I was sitting in his chair I did a calculation based on the information he gave me and I arrived at a grand total of around 200,000.

Ten years before I wrote this book, Achille became aware that he had become a curiosity, simply by not changing anything. Since Laglio became famous as the place George Clooney spends his summers and because Achille's shop is opposite George's villa, it became known that GC didn't get his hair cut in smart barber's shops in New York, Paris, Hollywood or London. No, he went to Achille's tiny shop, and for €12 ($13.30) a time, sometimes including a glass of wine from the bar next door, he could hang out with Laglio's card playing old boys. When the story was reported in the local press, a top fashion magavine desperate to find any snippets of news about George, sent a journalist and a photographer to Achille's shop and when the article came out, complete with a full-page photograph of Achille holding his scissors and revealing to the outside world who cut George's hair and where, the story began appearing in other magazines. After that, journalists from around the world would arrive, asking him to pose for a photograph and if, by the way, he had any gossip about George they could print. Achille may well have had, but he has been in business long enough to know how to be tactful when it comes to revealing information about his clients, so the journalists would go away with nothing except what was in the original article.

On another occasion when I was in Achille's chair he opened a draw to the right of the sink, revealing at least a dozen well known glossy mags, all with the article about him being Clooney's barber. When I asked him how much he had received in payment for granting permission, he said he'd received nothing. So I told him that the next time anyone came hustling, to tell them to hang on while he telephones me, and I will arrive within ten minutes to sort out a contract for him.

A couple of years ago I designed and hand painted a sign in the old fashioned style to go above Achille's shop door. It was to replace a sign that had flaked and faded to the point where it was illegible. The sign I did featured the traditional red and white diagonal strips of the barber with the word *Barbiere* across it in green. A few months after it had been in place Achille told me it must be the most photographed shop sign of all time, because every tourist to the village seemed to want to photograph his antiquated shop front, preferably with him standing in the doorway.

When we lived in Moltrasio, we got to know everybody

in the village. It was commonplace to be invited to lunch at our friends Enzo and Ada's house. Ada would take a large handful of home made pasta and plunge it into a cauldron of boiling, salted water that would be swinging above a roaring brushwood fire. Then she would stand over it, making sure it didn't soften beyond the imperative al dente state. She would then take the pasta and add it a tomato, onion and basil sauce laced with grated goat's cheese. Meanwhile her husband would fill a large earthenware jug with half decent Barbera - a local red wine - from a large demijohn that would be resting on two blocks of wood on his cantina floor.

Enzo and Ada invited Nicola and I to lunch so many times I cannot begin to count them, but on each occasion they did it was always one to appreciate because they would recount stories about the past ways of Italian life. To get to their house from ours was quite a strain on the leg muscles, because it overlooked the main village and the climb to get there seemed to go on for a lot longer than the thirty minutes it actually took. I recall walking past one particular house on the way up there. The inhabitants lived on the first floor and their farm animals were kept on the ground floor. The floorboards were spaced a centimetre apart so the warmth from the animals rose up through the gaps to warm the people.

It was by coincidence rather than planning that our arrival in Italy enabled us, for a decade to experience the remnants of the old Italian lifestyle and it was both educational and heart-warming. From then on, many laws have unhinged centuries of culture and they have not been helped by the introduction of the Internet, the EU or Satellite TV. Of course what is continuing to take place here affects every other country and before long there will be little difference. We will be one unhappy mass, devoid of tradition. Fortunately for us two the residents of Argegno have recently elected (in our opinion) the best

Mayor we've ever come across. He is efficient, practical and intelligent, and although at thirty-two he is still a young man, he is of the old school, so our immediate future is in safe hands, as he is as keen as the residents are to keep the community spirit of Argegno as un-spoilt as possible, for as long as possible. Since he was elected an example of his work has been to revive an Italian tradition of providing a free, five-course Christmas lunch for pensioners, plus generous prizes to be won in a free Tombola. 30 per cent of the 600 inhabitants of Argegno are sixty-five or over, so it is no mean undertaking.

Nowadays, when I'm in the company of younger Italians I must bore them rigid, because I try to make them aware of what we as foreigners appreciate most about the Italian way of life. Then I try to convince them to do everything they can to preserve it because once its gone it will never return. From experience I tell them that if what they know disappears, then the rest of their lives will be spent looking for contentment they will never find.

15 Bed and Breakfast

When we bought the villa in Argegno in 2004, our initial intention had been to stay in the one bedroom apartment in Moltrasio, which had my art studio underneath and, being in the main square it was a good site to attract custom. To help cover the higher rents due on the studio and the apartment, we thought we would rent the villa to tourists. It would also be an investment for the future. This changed when Nicola suddenly announced that she wanted to live in the villa, because she thought it was such a fantastic place.

I also wanted to live in the villa, so seven months after we'd completed the purchase, we moved in. Why it took so long wasn't as you might expect in Italy, because of some unforeseen bureaucracy, but because it took me that long to decorate it inside and out, paint the almost infinite amount of railings that surround the balconies and terraces and for the tradesmen we'd hired to update it and eventually to furnish it. The snag was, now we'd moved from Moltrasio, I'd lost the prime location that enabled me to sell my paintings to passing tourists and we were still in the process of trying to get planning permission to create a studio in the villa. So, to compensate for the loss in income, Nicola had another bright idea, which was to turn part of the villa into a bed and breakfast. The villa was certainly big enough for a B&B and in addition there was a self-contained one-bedroom apartment on the first floor, with a stunning view of the lake. We decided we would give it a go, so from being a professional artist I became a domestic, with Nicola agreeing to help out at weekends with the mass of washing and ironing, bed making and the steam-cleaning of the tiled floors. Needs must, as they say, so if we wanted to continue living in a beautiful home then we would have to work to keep it.

The B&B is a British institution and lots of them exist in the countryside and seaside towns. They are a more modern version of the guest houses where working class people used to stay in the last century when holidayed in places like Blackpool. As the name suggests, they offer overnight accommodation with breakfast included in the price. They are for the most part very individualistic (and offer far more comfort, and a welcome than the old guest house landladies ever did!), which apart from being economically priced, is part of their appeal.

A typical bed and breakfast will be in a private house, where two or three of the otherwise spare bedrooms would be let out to guests, and it may be operated either as a primary or secondary source of income. Generally, guests will have the use of a private bedroom with either a private or en suite bathroom. Larger places may offer a small suite of rooms. Some older B&Bs have private bedrooms with a bathroom that is shared with other guests. Breakfast is usually served in the host's kitchen or a designated dining area. Usually the owners prepare the breakfast and clean the rooms, although some bed and breakfast owners hire professional staff to do it. However, a property that hires professional management is no longer considered a bed and breakfast and enters the category of an inn or hotel.

After our initial layout for bedding, towels, dressing

gowns, hair dryers, crockery and furniture we advertised the facilities on the Internet. The first year was slow, but the second year was a lot busier. B&B is seasonal and at best it lasts for seven months of the year. The holiday season in Italy usually starts a week after Easter and runs until mid-October. To the outsider, running a bed and breakfast abroad can seem like an appealing way to earn some money. They believe that the owners can live in a country they love and be their own boss while working from home. They mistakenly assume that running a B&B is a simple matter of putting some bread in the toaster and making a pot of tea or coffee, then relaxing for the rest of the day, but that's not how it is. Running a B&B during the season is a full time job and I soon found out that if I didn't give it my all we wouldn't make much money. It is often uneconomical to pay someone to do the domestic work, because there are usually only a small number of rooms to let out. To remain competitive with hotels, the prices need to be kept keen and thus the profit margin will be low, so the only way for us to run a B&B and make it worthwhile was to do everything ourselves. I have to say it was some of the most concerted work I've ever done, but as it was seasonal I knew that when November arrived I would be able to take it easy. We gave a personal, welcoming service as well as offering keen prices, and of course we had that spectacular view. All these things made us popular, and as word of mouth spread, we became very busy.

The concept of a B&B was unknown to the majority of Italians in the Como area, who have traditionally stayed in a hotel or have rented a villa or apartment, so when we started we had little competition locally, and we did rather well. However, there were indications that the economy was stagnating and that it was not likely to improve for a long time. A weekly TV magazine programme put on a feature that offered solutions for homeowners to help them make ends meet. One of the articles offered viewers advice on how to start a B&B. The phrase "bed & breakfast" is obviously English, because that was where it began and because only a small percentage of Italians were aware of it, the programme needed to explain it fully. Italians could understand the literal translation - *letto e colazione* - but they still didn't understand what it meant in practice. Possibly the reason bed and breakfast was relatively unknown in Italy, especially in the villages, is because friends and family are likely to live in the same town or village and within walking distance of each other, if not next door. Thus there has never been the necessity to have a spare room or two to put guests up, because they would return home after visiting.

If you run a business in Italy, it's more than likely you'll need a licence. No doubt this was one of the reasons why there were so few, if any B&Bs, because a householder who might have been considering starting a B&B would have been deterred by the bureaucracy. Then, courses on how to run a B&B started to be held in Milan and other places, and now there are a hundred B&Bs around Lake Como, compared to five when we started. Nonetheless, for a while we discovered we had the advantage over a B&B run by Italians, because most of the foreign visitors to the lakes are English speakers and know very little, if any Italian, so we could answer all queries without having to ask, say, a neighbour's eleven-year-old child who happened to be studying English to translate. However, for the Italians to get over the language problem the B&B courses advised them to join web sites that offered to answer enquiries by phone or e-mail via an automated booking system. The problem with this system is that if there is no personal contact with a B&B owner, the tourist cannot assess the standard of their host's English, and often when they arrive they can find that they are unable to communicate with their hosts during their stay.

Soon after we started our B&B, if I met an Italian I knew and they asked me for my latest news update, I'd tell them what we were doing. B&B had become one of the latest topics and when they found somebody who was actually running one they wanted to know more. After I'd outlined what we provided, they'd say, 'let me get this straight; you have people staying in your home that you have never met before. You don't know anything about them and they are foreigners. Are you mad?' And as far as breakfast is concerned, I've said before that all Italians need in the morning is an espresso before they leave the house as fast as possible. So precisely what, our enquirers wanted to know was, what did we give these foreigners for breakfast, and in what quantities? I would then tell them that four to six people may sit at the breakfast table, and because some people consider breakfast to be the main meal of the day it can take them an hour to consume the array of different foods and drinks we provided. They were amazed at this, and even more so at how people can eat so much and so early, and drink so many pots of coffee. They would ask, 'non si rendono conto che caffè è un lassativo? Essi devono essere recarsi in bagno tutta la mattina dopo! (Don't they realise that coffee is a laxative? They must be going to the toilet all morning after it!)'

After we'd been running the B&B for a couple of years, a guest said to us that we must like people! I guess they are right, but until then, we'd never given it a thought. We had no previous experience of it at all, but traits like friendliness, consideration, a warm atmosphere, a decent breakfast and the English language helped to make our business stand out from the crowd and many guests came back year after year. A B&B relies heavily on word of mouth recommendation, as well as web sites like Tripadvisor. Tripadvisor has become the Gospel and guests tell us about other places they have stayed where the owners have begged them to write a good review about them, because they know it is essential for future business. Having a good rating can seriously boost the profile of a B&B and we had excellent reviews from kind guests who gave us a five-star rating. When we decided to start a B&B we believe we did it for the right reasons, and that was to provide good value in a pricey area. We decided early on we weren't interested in accommodating guests for just one night, so we specified two nights as the minimum. This was because we wanted a certain amount of job satisfaction, which we would get by getting to know the people we had staying in our home. In fact, on average most people stayed for three or four nights and if they stayed in *il mono locale*, the self-contained apartment on the first floor they would stay for a week, if not two. We made the price for the apartment attractive by offering seven nights for the price of six, which included breakfast delivered to the door at whatever time the guests wanted it. This made the apartment the best value for money on the entire lake.

We've had guests stay that have made our experience as B&B owners interesting and highly enjoyable and we still keep in contact with some of them and a few of them have become friends. Our guests have included doctors, nurses, photographers, civil servants, travel writers, teachers, policemen, textile designers, government officials, farmers, child welfare workers, bankers, a meteorologist, a theatrical agent, a fireman, an Irish footballer, a Russian estate agent and a London cabbie. We've also had a few Italians staying with us, but as the B&B culture is still relatively unknown to them and they don't require a hearty breakfast, they gave us the impression that they thought we were a *pensione*, a lodging house or hostel.

However, despite our efforts to build our reputation of a new business there were occasional, unexpected reality checks, not least in respect of the time dedicated to looking after guests' personal needs, the need to be polite at all times and having to put up with lie-ins. I've read articles in magazines where couples who intend to start a B&B to supplement their pensions when they retire, ask readers for advice. Those replying said that it was some of the hardest work they have ever done and retirement age was most definitely NOT the right time to start. Being open-minded is another big must. In some countries it is illegal to turn customers away based on race, religion or sexual preference. If we took issue with things like that, running a B&B wouldn't have been for us.

One mistake you can make is to assume that all your guests are heterosexual and (hopefully) monogamous. Some of the nicest guests we had, and possibly the most amusing (especially after the anecdotes they told us) were two gay men and two lesbians, who were travelling together. They were all hairdressers from Chicago and all were in their mid-forties. They had booked for three nights and on meeting them I assumed they were two traditional married couples. However, when I escorted them to their bedrooms, the two men went into one bedroom and the two women went into the other one. We were so delighted by their humour that on the last evening of their stay, we decided to hold a dinner party, and after it was over, one of the men cut Nicola's hair. The evening after they left, an Australian heterosexual couple arrived and the husband's face dropped when I told him that two gays had been sleeping in the bed the night before. 'I wish you hadn't told me that!' He said. More often than not, it pays to be the model of discretion.

Soon after the Australians had gone we had a South African couple staying. They were around the thirty-year-old mark and looked very fit, but they didn't say much and they looked fed up when they arrived. He was a brusque type and didn't even say hello. When I showed them to their bedroom, he went straight to the bed and stripped off all the bedclothes. While he was in the process of destroying my hard work, his girlfriend said that he'd had bad experiences in the past with bed bugs. Because they were staying in the self-contained apartment I didn't see them for a couple of days, but I bumped into them on one of the terraces. The boyfriend continued on his way, but the girlfriend stopped and seemed as if she wanted to chat. She then unfolded a story about them getting on the ferry without buying tickets, and when the ticket inspector came along, they locked themselves inside the toilet to avoid him. She seemed proud to tell me that they then sneaked into the top flight, five-star, Grand Hotel Villa Serbelloni in Bellagio and went swimming in the pool without permission, then used the towels and the loungers and helped themselves to the canapés. When one of the hotel attendants became suspicious of them and asked them what their room number was, they invented one, and when he went off to check them out, they dressed as quickly as possible and ran off before he came back.

A couple of delightful Canadians stayed with us for three nights. They were on their honeymoon, but were taking it before they actually married. They'd changed the date of the ceremony because some of their guests couldn't make it, and as they had already booked the honeymoon they postponed the wedding. The peculiarity about these two was, before they came to us they had stayed at the Hotel Villa d'Este in Cernobbio. One of Italy's forty-eight UNESCO heritage sites, it is situated some fifteen kilometres north of Argegno and was built in the sixteenth century by a Cardinal as his private summer palace. After him, it was owned by a succession of aristocrats and converted into a hotel in 1876. It's one of the most expensive hotels in the world and a place where celebrities stay because it guarantees them anonymity.

When the two Canadians booked the three nights with us they mentioned that they would be staying at the Hotel Villa d'Este beforehand. Nicola wrote back, asking if they were sure they hadn't made a mistake; why would they want to stay with us after residing in one of the world's most luxurious hotels? They booked nevertheless, and over hospitality drinks on the evening they arrived, we asked them just what it was like to reside in five-star-luxury. They said it was like living in an antique shop of the highest quality. In their bedroom was an abundance of eighteenth century furniture, covered in gold leaf and trimmed with deep crimson velvet. The floors were of intricately inlaid mosaic hardwoods blocks, strewn with Persian silk rugs. Delicate, hand-embroidered lace-curtains hung at all the windows, which overlooked the glory of the lake. Half a dozen Venetian chandeliers hung from the ceilings, including one in the bathroom. To complete the picture, the most important item in their bedroom was a French oak four-poster bed, and above it an impressive hand carved, gold-leafed pelmet, swathed in metres of crimson shot silk, interwoven with a gold thread.

Their honeymoon was scheduled for the last week in April, and they had managed to find an early season special offer at the hotel for bed and breakfast at €1,000 a night, but they said that even at that price they didn't receive the quality of service they imagined they would. The breakfast on the first morning was outstanding and so was the service, but for the next two mornings they were placed at the back of the dining room and they found the sugar and the condiments missing from their table, but they were too far away to attract the attention of any waiters, and so had to get them themselves. They also found that when they booked a time to go swimming in the heated outdoor pool, their names were on two of the loungers but there were no towels provided and there was nobody around to ask for them, so they had to go back to their bedroom to get some. They said they far preferred their stay with us, because we took care of their every need and actually spoke to them, whereas at the hotel they said they hadn't found another person to speak to in three days. What I remember most about their story was that they said there were no prices on anything displayed for sale in the hotel. Apparently, if hotel guests want to buy something, they just point to what they want and pay for it when they leave, regardless of how much it cost.

After the Canadians, two South African Boers arrived

with their wives. They were ex-rugby professionals and they towered above me. The women were pretty large too, and I hoped when I saw them that the beds could take their weight. In the evenings the two men would sit on the balcony overlooking the lake. They'd brought with them a dozen or so bottles of South African whisky that they had been carrying around Europe in a canvas hold-all. They invited us to drink some with them after their wives had gone to bed, but it was too strong for us. The bag must have been a lot lighter when they went, because they left plenty of empty bottles!

They were firm nationalists and since retiring from rugby they'd acquired homesteads. They told us stories about having to protect their properties at night from marauding herds of wild animals and also from robbers, because out in the wilds, there was nobody else to do it. If they were sitting drinking whisky on their unlit verandahs and heard a noise in the bush, they would fire their rifles in the direction of it, even though it was pitch dark. Next morning they would take a walk to see if they had hit anything. Sometimes it would be a man, whom they would assume was a robber.

We had two German couples staying, at different times. They, like the Italians didn't understand about British style B&Bs, because when they arrived they were carrying trays of food and they asked us where the fridge was. We didn't let people use our kitchen, but we had to on this occasion because there had obviously been a misunderstanding and they had thought we were a hostel. After that we made sure our web site stated we were not a hostel and did not allow self-catering in the B&B rooms. We didn't get any more requests for accommodation from Germans after that.

We had another misunderstanding with six Americans, who had booked for three nights and had arrived on the doorstep believing they had rented the whole apartment for themselves for €70 per night. Naturally they were surprised to find that we lived there! In this area a three - bedroom apartment costs three times that amount per night, and for a minimum of a week. They said the reason for the misunderstanding was because they'd been travelling around Europe for some months, either renting apartments or staying in hotels and B&Bs and they had forgotten what they had booked by the time they got to us.

We've had guests arrive on the doorstep who have been travelling around Europe for such a long period of time they had become so disorientated that they didn't know what part of Italy they were in. We've had others arrive who have said they didn't even know what country they were in. A single Italian-American male who stayed with us was trying to locate the village where his ancestors originated. He was certain they came from Argegno and he was staying with us because I could speak Italian and I might be able to help him find them. I thought it would be a simple task of looking through the telephone book for his family name but it wasn't that easy. He had me spending an hour in the Municipio, looking through the records of the inhabitants of Argegno going back over three hundred years, but we found nobody with the names he had given me. Not to be deterred, he intended to visit every Municipio along the lake in the hope that he would be able to locate where his origins lay. Fortunately he didn't ask me to accompany him.

An Indian married couple from Delhi, both architects had booked a three-night stay with us some months ahead. When I opened the front door to them I was slightly alarmed to see that the wife was heavily pregnant. She told me that this was going to be their last holiday for some time! She was actually eight months gone and I was worried in case she delivered prematurely, and even more so when, just before they went to bed, she asked if I could look-up the telephone number of the emergency services in case she needed an ambulance. Fortunately an emergency call wasn't necessary.

An American couple who had enjoyed the day riding on the ferryboats that criss-cross the lake had a problem on their way back. The husband had got off the boat at Argegno, but the wife hadn't, because she got talking to someone she'd met on the boat and had become distracted. The husband arrived at our villa in a panic because he didn't know how he was ever going to find her again. Because he didn't speak any Italian, he had me telephoning all the numbers of all the boat stops on the way to Como for the next hour in the hope that his wife had got off the boat and he could go and pick her up in his hire car, but nobody answered. I thought that when the boat docked in Como she would be able to get the next boat back, but according to the timetable there wasn't one. At this news the husband flapped even more, because he said he was sure she would never find the village or our villa on her own. I finally got through to the Como terminus and with the husband's help I described to the person on the other end of the line what his wife looked like and what she was wearing, but they told me there was nobody there of that description. To assuage the husband's anxiety, I said surely she would have the ability to get a taxi back to Argegno. He said she wouldn't know what to tell the driver, because she could not pronounce the name of the village. The majority of our guests would pronounce the name of the village incorrectly and I had already given this woman that was lost a one-to-one in how to pronounce Argegno but she hadn't been do it to save her life. She said "Ajeejeenio", "Arjeneegio" or "Arjeegengano", but never "Ar-jen-yo". Fortunately for me, an hour later the crisis evaporated when she arrived by car as if nothing had happened. The person she'd been talking to on the boat knew somebody who was able to organise a lift with somebody else who lived in Argegno who spoke some English and happened to know where our villa was.

The self-contained apartment became very popular

because it had a fully equipped kitchen, where guests could cater for themselves if they chose. It was necessary to allow for wear and tear, because when people cooked they sometimes broke china and glass. These incidents had to be accepted as accidents, but cigarette burns in sheets were not, and they were only discovered when guests had left. We sometimes found stains from coffee, waterproof mascara, foundation and lipstick on pillow cases, which were tiresome but not too difficult to remove, but removing spilt nail varnish was virtually impossible. One of the most costly stains was a burn mark on a new cream bedspread, which apparently was caused by a hot hair dryer. The most expensive damage we found was after a week's stay by a young Filipino couple. When they had gone I discovered a wooden windowsill had been snapped in half. It was irreparable, and how it had happened is still a mystery, because it was too high off the floor and too narrow to sit on. They had also placed one of the coloured candles we provided on top of the television and let it drip wax all over the back of the television. They had also ruined a cotton tablecloth, again from candle wax and in the kitchen I found a large chip out of the lip of the ceramic sink. This was also irreparable and had to be replaced.

Italian culture can have some interesting effects on foreign visitors. We have some rather kitsch stone statues in the garden that we inherited from the previous owners. One of the statues is a half-naked lady. There are also some partly-clad cherubs that flank the outside stairs and they happened to be in the publicity photographs we posted on our web site to advertise our B&B. Statues like this are a common sight in Italy and their origins are ancient, both Greek and Roman. The practice of sculpting them was revived in the Renaissance and Italians take little notice of them in their daily lives. However, because our statues were featured on our web site, we had an enquiry asking us if we were a nudist B&B, and if we were, the enquirer wanted to stay for a month. It would be easy for us to scoff at the mind-set of some guests but it was important for us to remember that some people had never been out of their own country before. For them, being plunged into a foreign environment where almost everything is different and where English is not widely spoken can be quite daunting. There were others who had never been to Europe before and for them, the whole experience was surreal and sometimes difficult. We remember what it was like for us when we first arrived in Italy, so when they thought they had found somebody who was sympathetic to their plight they tended to rely on us.

But speaking the world's most prevalent language was not always beneficial for business, because when the guests actually arrived, some of them were aching to speak to someone who could understand them. For some curious reason we seemed to be a magnet for the type of guest who had encountered a problem in another part of Italy and they needed our help to sort it out. Nicola has contacts within the Italian authorities through her work in Milan, so she knows what to do and who to contact if a guest has a problem and it has sometimes been necessary for her to do so, otherwise they would have been in deep trouble. During our B&B years it was not unusual for Nicola to come home from Milan, then spend two hours on the phone solving a guest's dilemma. Some of them expected it as part of the service, but little did they realise that they had landed on their feet, because they could have been staying at a B&B were the owners didn't speak any English, nor had the capability or the means to sort it out for them. A lot of tourists expect everybody to speak English as if it's the only language on the planet. They seem puzzled and can get annoyed, impatient and disrespectful if they don't. We've had guest's who have said they would be glad to get back home, because they were tired of trying to make themselves understood. Some of the older ones have said they would never holiday anywhere but in an English-speaking country again.

I've mentioned a few times that the average Italian rarely has more than an espresso and a cigarette for breakfast. A decent B&B should serve a substantial continental breakfast, which should include a choice of fruit juice, fresh fruit salad, yoghurt, cereal, bread, butter, milk, cold meats, cheeses, brioche, jams, and an unlimited amount of tea and coffee. A lot of B&Bs in Italy just serve a cup of coffee and a brioche. We had several guests tell us about their experiences in other B&Bs. They also told us that by comparison we didn't charge enough. For instance, there are a substantial number of B&Bs in Italy who will hand guests a plastic token for breakfast, which they are expected to present at the counter of a bar across the road in exchange for a cappuccino and a brioche. This arrangement saves the B&B owner hours of work, energy and costs over a season, but guests are unlikely to return or pass on recommendations.

We had guests who told us they had to pay extra for their breakfast, even though the bed and breakfast they stayed in advertised itself as a bed and breakfast. Others said, their B&B was like a youth hostel, where the breakfast was minimal, they had single beds, and they had to queue in the morning to share the bathroom with strangers. We had some who stayed in a B&B in Rome where only one hand-towel per person was provided and there was no soap. When they asked for soap they had to pay for it. In the familiar tourist centres, particularly in the cities, and where millions of people go every year to see the art galleries and museums, B&B owners are not very particular in how they treat their guests because they know they are guaranteed business.

When we have a break ourselves to see other parts of Italy, we always stay in B&Bs if we can. We decided to visit the region of Umbria, and stayed there for four days and nights. We chose a B&B that wouldn't have been in business without the assistance of technology, because without a reliable satnav we wouldn't have found it. It was set in a farmer's field, at the end of very pot-holed track with no signs and no street lighting. There was nobody else staying there and possibly this was because it was expensive. The owners didn't speak English, which didn't concern us, but it made me wonder how they got their business. Also the breakfast was inconsistent. It started well on the first day and there was plenty of it, but it was as if preparing it for four successive mornings was too much effort, or perhaps they ran out of food, and we ended up with just the predictable cappuccino and a brioche. We booked another B&B, this time for three nights in Puglia. It was full of screaming kids. The breakfast consisted of a large homemade jam tart that was in the fridge when we arrived, but was supposed to last us for three mornings. Coffee was also available, provided we made it. We stayed in a B&B in Naples for three nights, which was run by a sweet old lady. It was a little on the expensive side, but it amused me; the breakfast was fresh and in one way it was everything we expected a B&B breakfast to be; beautifully presented in the demure, old fashioned British way with paper doilies, linen napkins and a silver service, but the proportions were tiny. There just wasn't enough for the both of us.

On another holiday we spent four nights on the Calabrian coast. We had a decent sized bedroom, but it wasn't cheap. We arrived in the late evening and the weather was blissfully warm, so at bedtime we left the window wide open. At seven-thirty in the morning construction work started on the house next door so we couldn't be accused of being lie-ins. When we went for breakfast, there didn't appear to be any, but the Italian owner asked us what we would like for the rest of our stay. We asked him what he provided for breakfast.

He said, 'How about a brioche and a cappuccino?'

'Good,' we replied.

'Okay,' he said, 'tomorrow I will drive to the bakers and buy you a brioche each, and then I will come back and make you a cappuccino.'

I felt like saying, 'BIG DEAL!' but I received a look from Nicola that I know only too well, which made me keep my mouth shut.

When Nicola had to go to Rome for work purposes she used to stay in the same B&B, which has closed now because the lady who ran it decided to retire. She would only have guests in her home that she knew, or ones that had been recommended to her by people she knew. Nicola had met the lady's son through her work and he had introduced her to his mother.

The majority of our B&B guests have been Australian. This was because the Australian dollar was strong against the Euro at the time and consequently they took the opportunity to travel in Europe. We were often told that we had been selected particularly because they knew they would get a decent pot of tea, with milk and sugar, because English style tea isn't an Italian forte. For over a hundred years the prestige of Lake Como has made it a holiday destination for wealthy Americans, but since the advent of mass tourism the number of middle-income Americans visiting Italy has overtaken the wealthy ones, and they are our second most numerous overseas visitors. I've never been sure that Americans understand what an English style B&B is all about. They don't, to my knowledge have B&Bs like we do, but they do have motels, which in general do not include breakfast in their overnight tariff, or even have a dining area. So, when Americans arrive to stay with us they don't always connect with what we do. However, by the time they were ready to leave most of them had got the point and we have never had any complaints, especially if they had previously been staying in an Italian run B&B, because that had completely confused them. We liked having Brits stay because they understood about a traditional B&B, but oddly, over the seasons we didn't get as many as we did Australians or Americans. This was due in the main to the fact that a lot of Brits prefer Spain to Italy, or they go to Venice, Rome or Florence in preference to the lakes.

Generally the B&B guests of all nationalities we had were great, but there were some who needed looking after beyond the call of duty, because they considered themselves to be the only guests we'd ever had. They wanted four-star treatment on the cheap, and sometimes we became their itinerary organisers as well as their hosts. Before Wi-Fi became available, if they wanted information they would spend hours looking for it on my computer. On occasions there would be a queue of guests waiting for their turn to work on their holiday, contact their relatives, update their blogs or use the printer to run off documents and maps. In fact I had to buy a laptop so I could work without having to move aside for guests who said they had a desperate need for a computer. There wasn't an Internet café in Argegno, so as soon as Wi-Fi came to Italy we had it installed so that guests could look for what they wanted on their tablets and iPads.

Because we lived on the premises, we had by default made ourselves too accessible. If a guest had a query or a problem they would automatically look for one of us to sort it out for them. One of the most frequent requests we had was to book tickets for them to go and see Leonardo da Vinci's mural, *L'Ultima Cena*, The Last Supper, in the refectory of the convent of Santa Maria della Grazie in Milan. This mural is so popular that the people running the booking office say that tickets have to be booked two months in advance if people want to be sure of seeing it. This news came as a great disappointment to some of our guests and so they would ask us if we could pull strings to get them tickets, which of course we could not do. And trying to get a booking office clerk to pick up the phone so we could ask if there were any cancellation tickets could mean being put on hold for ages.

Translation of documents, brochures and timetables and organising boat, bus and train schedules so they could visit other parts of Europe were tasks outside of what we officially offered, and yet we regularly found ourselves doing them for our guests. We also found ourselves downloading and printing boarding passes for plane flights, suggesting the best local restaurants, booking a table for them by telephone, telling them what to eat and the correct wines to go with it, writing this information down in Italian on a scrap of paper so they could show the waiter what they wanted, and last but not least drawing them a map so they could find the restaurant.

Because of the language problem certain guests were having, we sometimes had to tell them how to renew their out-of-date passports so they could get home. We had a woman staying who lost her passport, so Nicola informed her of the procedure and documentation she would require to enable her to get a temporary one from her Consulate, and get it delivered by courier so she wouldn't have to interrupt her holiday by travelling to Milan to get it. We've had guests arrive without their luggage because it wasn't on the plane when they landed at Malpensa and we had to telephone the airport every few hours to track it, lend them clothes, toothbrushes and washing materials, then correspond with the courier service to have it forwarded to the next place they were travelling to in Italy after they had left us. We've had guests who have stayed with us, then travelled to another part of Italy to continue their holiday who have, some weeks later come across a problem they cannot solve and they have telephoned us to help them sort it out. We've had guests leave Argegno making sure they are armed with our telephone numbers in case we can be useful to them if they come unstuck. We've even had people we don't know, and who have never been guests send an email via our web site, pleading for help to sort a dilemma out because we happened to be the only ones they had found who live in Italy who speak English.

Another type of enquiry I learnt to avoid were the ones that were from artists who wanted to meet me to talk about art. It usually meant they weren't artists at all and they just wanted company.

It sounds miserable of me, but I've actually hidden from some guests because they wanted to occupy too much time chatting about whatever it was that was preoccupying them. But I cannot hide all the time and when I have reappeared they have been waiting for me. I should imagine it is easy for staff in a hotel to get away from their guests, because they can invent an urgent phone call, but because I was in my own home with nowhere to run, I often found myself praying for the day when they left.

I've also spent a considerable amount of time packing and posting articles guests had left behind by mistake; assisted in the touching-up of damaged paintwork on a rental car; repaired guests shoes, jewellery, handles on holdalls, castors on cases and broken sunglasses; located and bought special foods and liquids for guests on medication and provided medicines for guests with headaches, colds and flu and bandages for sprained ankles and other minor injuries. Patience and a sense of humour is required by a B&B owner, but when running one it is important to set some limits. There were parts of the villa where we didn't want guests to go. One of them was in the kitchen, but some of the guests went there all the same. We had guests who wanted to help us make their breakfast. We had others who would pop in for a lengthy chat while we were trying to make it. We even had guests who started to make their own breakfast without our knowledge.

After a few disappointing experiences with some guests who never seemed to get out of bed, we decided to stipulate on the standard letter we sent to them that breakfast would be finished by 9.30 and rooms had to be vacated by 11 o'clock, or they wouldn't be tidied. The problem could be that some guests, especially the jet–lagged ones would be dead to the world and would sleep right through the determined time. When they did eventually wake, at whatever hour of the day it was they still expected their breakfast and to have their room tidied. We also had to stipulate that on their last day the room or rooms had to be vacated by 11 o'clock or they would be charged for an extra night. We had to insist on that, because we needed enough time to clean and prepare the rooms for the next round of guests. It's surprising how we never had an individual or a group of people not make the 11 o'clock deadline when they believed they would have to pay more, however tired they might have been.

We did guests' laundry for them. We used to do it for free, but later we had to make a minimum charge because guests started to abuse the privilege. Some guests even saved their dirty washing until they came to stay with us, as they'd heard from other guests that we did it for nothing. In Italy very few B&Bs will do their guests' laundry or allow it to be done on the premises, apart from hand washing. Hotels provide a laundry service but it is expensive: For example to wash a pair of socks a hotel will charge €2 and to wash and press a pair of jeans costs €5. Washing and ironing a shirt costs €7. We charged €6 for an 8kg load and we provided an iron and ironing board. Before we started charging for the use of our washing machine, it would be full all day with guests' personal washing and we weren't able to do our own washing or the bedding and towels we used in the B&B. Strangely, when we made a charge for the use of the machine, the amount of it halved, but we noticed our guests would do a lot more hand washing, because we didn't make a charge for that.

In Italy it is against the law to cook food in a B&B without a restaurant licence, and obtaining one of those would be prohibitively expensive. Only ready made foods, such as brioche and bread from the bakers and processed foods such as cheese and yogurt are allowed. Fresh fruit salad is allowed, but not bacon and eggs because if a tourist becomes ill and needs a doctor they might be questioned about what and where they ate while they had been on holiday.

Tips were minimal during the time we were in business as a B&B. I think we received seven in all and yet people feel obliged to leave a hefty tip in a trattoria or restaurant after every meal they have, when they had already been charged a 6 per cent *coperto* (cover charge) on their bill. All the same, we did find the occasional bottle of wine beside the bed with a thank you note.

It's a sad fact of life that no matter how fantastic a B&B may be or how good the customer service is, there will be someone someday who doesn't appreciate it. Their felt that their day, their week or their holiday had been ruined and they were going to make the owners suffer. Unexpectedly, and we believe unjustly, we had a poor review that definitely did us damage. Fortunately, we had already decided that we were going to stop doing B&B at the end of the season during which it was posted, so although it was annoying at the time it wasn't over harmful. It was posted on the net by an odd couple from Connecticut, who turned out to be the guests from hell. They stayed for three nights, but it seemed like three weeks, and it was as if they had decided to stay with us with the sole intention of writing a poor review. They were in their late seventies and they were travelling through Europe for five weeks, by public transport and with heavy luggage. Moving it must have been a remarkable act of endurance. They never smiled, never showed any humour and never showed any warmth. It was as if they belonged to the land of the living dead. At breakfast they shared no conversation (which isn't unusual when people have been married for donkey's years and especially when they are eating), so I thought I'd try some friendly conversation, like asking what their plans were for the day or whether they needed any information. That didn't work. In fact it seemed to make them gloomier still. It was as if they belonged to some peculiar religion that insisted on upholding a vow of silence when eating.

We'd received their three-night reservation via a tour operator rather than from them directly. Some people employ operators to book and organise their entire holiday, and this one had said in her email that she wanted to book her clients in with us for three nights because she had read rave reviews about our B&B on Tripadvisor and on Rick Steve's web site.

The problems began the moment I went to the garden gate to help them with their luggage. I had replied by return to the agent's enquiry for accommodation with information of what we offered, and tried and tested travel directions by car or public transport, but the agent hadn't forwarded this information to her clients, so they'd had difficulty finding us. When they did arrive, their faces looked like thunder. There are three steep, narrow flights of steps up to the villa from the garden gate and because they were a complete surprise they didn't help their disposition. If they had received the standard letter, either directly or via the agent (or looked at our web site), they would have seen that right across the middle of the message, printed in red, our B&B wouldn't be suitable for people who are old, infirm or are carrying a lot of heavy luggage. This couple were all of those things.

When they got their breath back and I managed to calm them with a pot of sweet tea in the dining room, they began tearing their tour operator apart. They said that she had just had a baby and she was far more interested in looking after it than she was in looking after them. And it wasn't the first time on this particular trip that she had let them down. However, even though I insisted I wasn't to blame for their getting lost and that I had told the agent to forward our standard letter so they would know what we offered and how to find us, I got the impression they weren't convinced that I had sent it.

During the three days and nights they stayed, they didn't complain about anything directly to me, but they did two months later when they posted a review on Tripadvisor. They fairly slammed us, commenting on there not being any signs to the villa and the amount of steps they had to walk up and down because there wasn't an elevator; that the village was a five minute walk away for dinner and there was no courtesy car to take them there or pick them up; that we slept on the premises and that we had cats, that their personal bathroom smelt and also that the B&B wasn't an inn and I insisted on talking to them when they didn't want to be spoken to.

It was clearly the wife who wrote the review, because she mentioned that her husband had to carry their heavy bags up the stairs. She never mentioned that I helped him or that our cats disappear out of sight until guests have gone, especially when there are guests staying they don't like. What she also omitted was that the bathroom was cleaned every day and the prevailing smell was caused by her husband, who used it before she did. On the few occasions I had cause to speak to her while she was staying with us she rarely replied, but instead would physically shake. On the first occasion I saw it happen I thought she must have something medically wrong with her, but she stopped shaking once I'd stopped speaking to her. I thought it best to direct any questions to the husband, so as to save mutual embarrassment. My reaction to the Tripadvisor review when I first saw it was to answer it, but Nicola advised me against doing so because she said that the woman was obviously mental, and if I did get involved with her it was likely to intensify things and she might start writing more insane reviews on other web sites. Reluctantly I let it be, but what I would have said if I had written back would most definitely have given her the shakes.

As we had decided it was our last year of doing B&B,

the poor review had minimum impact on business, but if it had been posted a few years earlier it could have been the ruin of us. Once a review is in place on Tripadvisor's web site its there for as long as a business is in operation. We are not the only ones who suffer such injustices. Whether a review is a good one or a poor one there is nothing a proprietor can do to remove it, and Tripadvisor say they cannot remove any of them. I have a relative who bought a hotel in the UK and a lot of poor reviews had been posted on Tripadvisor when the previous owners were running it. My relatives contacted Tripadvisor telling them the hotel was under new management, but Tripadvisor wrote back saying they couldn't remove them because the people who wrote them had PIN numbers, so they couldn't access the reviewers' accounts. Business for my relatives was slow during the early years, but as they accumulated good reviews they pushed the inherited reviews down the list, making them less obvious. A poor review makes the hard work that has gone into building up a good reputation by helping people to enjoy their holiday count for little or nothing. The affair with the couple from Connecticut confirmed our decision to end the responsibility and the work of running a B&B, but make an easier income out of tourism.

What made us change our ideas were our observations of a Frenchman, whom I'd seen around the village but never met. I'd heard that he rented a series of apartments in the village, then sub-let to tourists, charging them top dollar. What I'd also heard that sounded very attractive was that he did nothing much to earn his living except take reservations. When his tenants arrived at one of his properties, he handed them the front door key, then went sunbathing at the lakeside lido for the rest of the day. He didn't have to get out of bed at six-thirty in the morning, seven days a week to prepare guests' breakfasts. He had neither washing up nor food shopping to do, no bedclothes to wash and iron, no bedrooms and bathrooms to tidy or beds to make, no rubbish to dispose of, no free hospitality drinks or snacks to provide and no customer service issues to worry about. In other words, he let his tenants do it themselves, and when they left, a group of local ladies went into the apartment to prepare it for the next clients. He had his overheads in the way of council rates, service bills and the cleaning ladies' wages and he paid for top positions on the main search engines, but it must have been worth his while, because he did very good business. He was the influence behind our decision to stop doing B&B and advertise the first floor apartment of our villa for rent during the holiday season. Then all I'd have to do, instead of working my butt off, is hand a key to our clients, wish them a pleasant stay in Argegno and go off to the lido to sunbathe for the rest of the day. And when our tenants have gone, we will get in a group of ladies to clean, do the laundry and make the beds up.

I don't spend all day at the lido and nor do I intend to, because although I appreciate the sun, I find lying motionless for hours on end rather boring. I still work as an artist, and the thing I enjoy doing most is producing watercolours and oil paintings of the lake. Renting out the apartment gives us an income that helps us to live in and maintain a beautiful villa with a fantastic view, including partaking in a lifestyle we love. After all, we came to Italy to live in a country where, as I said in my first book, An Italian Home 'every day brings joy to the soul.

To give you an idea of what helped us decide to forsake the B&B business and rent out our first-floor apartment, here are some examples pertaining to the varying nature, lack of travel experience and knowledge of some past guests.

We had a problem telling the taxi driver where to find you because he was Italian.

Why is Italy all steps and churches?

The public tourist boat was full of tourists!

It's inconsiderate of the shopkeepers to close in the afternoons because I needed to buy things. Siesta time should be banned!

Is there gas and electricity in Italy?

The view from your balcony is absolutely fabulous. I don't think I've ever seen a view so fabulous anywhere. I could just sit on your balcony and look at the view all day but I think if I lived here I would tire of it very quickly.

Do you have a Coke vending machine in your house?

The weather is too nice.

If we miss the last ferryboat from Como, can you arrange for another one to pick us up?

My husband snores at night. What do you suggest I do about it in case he keeps people awake?

If we buy a bottle of wine from you, how do we pay you?

We are jet-lagged and our internal clocks are haywire. Could we have our breakfast before we go to bed?

I prefer sleeping in a double bed to a single bed, but I'm afraid that if I do, I will end up getting pregnant.

There are too many foreigners in Italy for my liking.

We will only need a light breakfast in the morning because we have to leave early, so skip the orange juice.

When we flew into Germany we changed our dollars into euros. When we stayed in Switzerland we had to change our euros into Swiss francs. Now we are in Italy we have had to change them back into euros again. Switzerland should be made to toe the line.

When we stayed in Venice, it was so expensive we had to eat pizza all the time and we don't like pizza.

If we go up the mountain by cable car, does it mean we have to come down on it, because I hate coming down?

Italy would be great if it was more like home.

If we take the bus to Como, does it stop in Como?

Do Italians ever do any work?

Why do Italians talk with their hands? I cannot stand people who talk with their hands.

Does the pizzeria sell anything else besides pizza?

What do Italians around here do for a living?

We'd love to meet George Clooney. By chance do you have his phone number?

How many girl friends has George Clooney had?

I just love George Clooney. I hear he has a new girl friend. Is he going to marry this one?
(George Clooney owns a villa close to us, in Laglio and is of course now married)

What does the normal Italian have for breakfast?

I love all cats but not too many.

I love Italian ice cream. If I lived here all I would do is eat ice cream.

When I bought a silk scarf in Como the girl at the checkout didn't acknowledge me. She didn't even say, 'have a nice day.'

I dislike feeling at home when I'm abroad in case I want to stay.

Can we get a beer in the wine bar?

We understand the lake is very deep. Are there any monsters in it?

If we go swimming in the lake, is there anywhere to swim?

If we miss the last boat back from Bellagio is there anywhere you can recommend for us to eat?

If we hire a speedboat, what happens if it breaks down?

I was reluctant to buy a new suitcase because I'll only use it when I go on holiday.

Once you've seen all the cathedrals in Italy, you don't want to see any more.

My wife has scratched the hire car. Do you have any blue paint?

If the police or the customs should stop us, what should we say?

How old are the mountains around here?

For a special occasion some friends of ours told us about an awesome restaurant. We haven't got a special occasion but we want to visit it all the same but we cannot remember where it is. Do you know what it's called?

I don't speak any Italian but I speak a bit of German. Will the Italians understand me?

Don't you feel cut-off living in Italy?

Is there anywhere around here that celebrates the Fourth of July?

Is it legal to drive a right hand drive car in this country?

My wife has Italian parentage but the only time she speaks Italian is when she swears.

I'm from Washington DC so I know all about tourists.

Isn't Cernobbio (a select village near Como city) the place where the nuclear power station exploded? (He meant Chernobyl in Russia.)

16 Random Facts about Italy

In the rural areas of Italy, Italians display a respect for the other person and their property at all times. This is one of the reasons we like living here, because it makes for a caring society. It also means that theft in this part of the country is minimal, and if there is any it is usually perpetrated by outsiders.

In a village community of a few hundred people, honesty has to rule. If an Italian robbed one of his neighbours he would never be able to hold his head up again. Word would get around within minutes and from then on he'd be blackballed. Both in Moltrasio, where we lived for thirteen years and in Argegno, we've received telephone calls on a number of occasions from concerned neighbours, telling us that an unknown face has been seen roaming around areas of the village where the tourist is unlikely to go. As word spreads, doors and window shutters will be closed on private houses as the unknown person progresses along the street.

Petty theft is rare in villages, but professional thieves have been known to strike on occasions. They are attracted to this area because of its wealth, and if a resident should see mysterious chalk or lipstick marks on the pavement, a wall or a gatepost outside a house, it will arouse suspicions. Once again, the occupiers will receive a telephone call, telling them to take care and make sure everything is locked, because their property could have been "cased" for a robbery.

When the pros are involved, they do a thorough job. A few years ago, there was an impressive theft on a large house near the centre of Moltrasio. It was the second home of some wealthy Milanese and it must have been thoroughly evaluated by professional thieves before they emptied it of the antiques within. The owners only occupied the house for two weeks in August each year. For the rest of the year it was closed up, so the residents didn't suspect anything when a group of workmen in overalls began renewing drainpipes outside the house. They were in fact acting as a decoy while their cohorts inside the house removed the furniture and paintings and put them into a large, unmarked van that was parked outside the open front door. They must have possessed nerves of steel, because they went for lunch in a local trattoria, chatted to some of the customers, returned to work in the afternoon and again the next day, continuing to fill their van with everything of value.

~~~

Northern Italians can be very formal, but if the opportunity arises, this attitude can be got around and they are only too glad to relax. In the south, formality is upheld even more, and it is wise to respect it. Although neither Nicola nor I necessarily follow the Italians' rather rigid formality, we don't complain about it, because we like the way Italians in general uphold traditions. They don't like having to respond to change. They are not open to experimentation or quirky gimmicks, and anything that is new will have been tried and tested in other places in the world, long before they will allow it into their lives, and we support that. Like Italians, we respect traditional values, inasmuch as if something is new and it is likely to change Italy for the worse, or dilute respect, then we are not in favour of it. We, like they, do our utmost to keep Italy as it is, and not as large scale commerce would like it to be.

They say that what happens in America today will spread to the UK five years later, and to the rest of Europe five years after that. But if it tries to implant itself in Italy, it will take another ten years, and only then if it fits into the nation's traditions and lifestyle. To us this attitude, coupled with respect, are Italy's saving graces in the on-going battle against modernism that successive governments keep trying to introduce so they can compete financially with other countries, but few of its citizens see the point. From the outsider's viewpoint this attitude might seem to be counter-productive in the modern world, but what we have sensed in the time we've been in Italy is a feeling that the greater part of the population tries their hardest to hang onto the way things used to be for as long as they can. They realise they have to absorb modernism because of the economic pressures that are forced upon them, but given the choice they would rather not have to do so.

Besides being fun to be around, we believe the Italians have the balance of living just right. Soon after we emigrated to Italy, it dawned on me how much the country is steeped in a history that is still functioning today. It is everywhere and anybody who lives in Italy or has visited the country will always be conscious of it. Italians have learnt how to apply their vast history to everyday life. What is the point of history if we don't learn from it? In the UK, history is now deemed irrelevant, hence consecutive generations flounder.

But adherence to tradition - superstition even - can lead to some odd interpretations. For example, one of our neighbours will only have her hair done at the village hairdresser when a full moon is due, because she's convinced this phase of the lunar cycle makes her locks grow stronger and thicker. There is however an ancient Italian law that says hairdressers and barbers cannot open for business on Mondays, so if the full moon appears on a Monday and her hair needs doing, she will wait for the next lunar cycle to arrive.

In some ways, Italy has changed since the days when shops closed at one o'clock sharp for lunch and siesta and opened again at four o'clock in the afternoon, and when no store was allowed to open on a Sunday. Regulations that forbade greengrocers from selling sandwiches, or a shoemaker selling shirts and ties, or a butcher selling anything other than meat were removed in 2000. In a revolutionary step, the same law allowed shopkeepers to set their own hours within a thirteen-hour maximum working day and a few shops were even allowed to open on a Sunday. The new law was welcomed by the large stores and supermarkets, because they had been fighting parliament for decades for it, but the smaller shopkeepers, especially in villages like Argegno don't agree with the liberalisation and continue the way they always have. Some customers, as well as the foreign tourist wanted the change because before the law was altered they found it bemusing, if not frustrating to find that shops always seem to be closed. But when the tourist arrives in the rural areas they will find that nothing has changed. Most of the smaller shopkeepers saw the new liberalisation as harmful because they said it made people work too hard. They say they have a humane and pleasant way of life and they don't like being forced to compete.

'Italia' means "calf land."

Italy is one of the founder members of the European Union and the Group of Eight (G8). It is one of the world's most powerful nations.

Rome is the capital of Italy and is three thousand years old.

Rome is further north than New York City, yet it rarely snows in Rome.

The Italian language descended from Vulgar Latin, a dialect spoken during the last years of the Roman Empire, mixed with the Tuscan dialect, but every region in Italy speaks its own dialect that has little correlation to Italian.

There are two independent states within Italy: San Marino and the Vatican City. San Marino is the world's oldest republic. The official language of the Vatican is Latin.

The Vatican City is the only nation in the world that can lock its gates at night. It has its own phone company, radio and TV stations, stamps, money and an army, the Swiss Guard.

Milan is Italy's second largest city. It is the financial and fashion centre and the third most visited tourist destination in the country.

Italy's 59.7 million citizens have a life expectancy of 82.4 years, which is 2.1 years longer than the average European.

21.2 per cent of Italy's population is over 65 compared to 18.2 per cent elsewhere in the EU.

Italy's birth rate has been the lowest in the western world for the past fifteen years. Both political and church leaders have expressed concern and have offered rewards to couples that have more than one child.

Many single Italian children live at home until they are well into their thirties, even if they have a job.

The average disposable income of the Italian per annum is €23,000.

Italy's average unemployment rate is 12.6 per cent but it is as high as 20 per cent in the south.

Italy has a resident foreign population of 1.27 million.

Ninety per cent of Italians are Roman Catholic, but only thirty per cent attend church regularly.

In northern Italy surnames tend to end with an "i" whilst those in the south generally end with an "o." The most common Italian surname is Rossi.

50 million Italians left Italy between the country's unification in 1861 and the present day, a world record in mass migration.

The majority of Italian-Americans immigrants were from Naples and southern Italy.

There are two hundred thousand Italians living in the UK.

There are 80 million people alive in the world with Italian heritage.

There are twenty nine thousand British living in Italy. Most are retirees.

Three-quarters of the landmass of Italy is hilly or mountainous.

Italy has more volcanoes than any other European country. There are fourteen in all, the most famous being Mount Etna and Mount Vesuvius.

Italians suffer more earthquakes per year than other Europeans. This is because the Italian peninsula stands on a fault line.

The highest mountain peak in Europe, Monte Bianco (better known as Mont Blanc) is in Italy and is 4,572 metres (15,771 feet) high.

The thermometer is an Italian invention. So are eyeglasses, the battery, the espresso machine, the pianoforte, the typewriter, nitro-glycerine, the violin, the cello, wireless telegraphy and the ice-cream cone.

Bologna University is the oldest in Europe. It was founded in 1088 and it is still functioning.

The unit of electrical pressure, the volt is named after the Italian, Alessandro Volta. He was a pioneer in electricity, who was born in Como in 1745. The battery made by Volta is credited as the first electrochemical cell. There is a museum of his inventions in Como.

Italy claims to have taught the rest of Europe how to cook. The first cookbook is reputed to have been written in 1474 by Bartolomeo Sacchi, who was born in Piadena, near Cremona.

The oldest olive tree is in Umbria and is reportedly 1,700 years old.

The largest truffle ever found was near Pisa. It weighed 1.49 kilos (3.3lbs) and was sold at auction for €28,000.

Italy is the largest producer of wine in the world. The average Italian consumes 280 litres (seventy-four gallons) of wine a year.

The average Italian consumes 40kg (88 pounds) of pasta per year.

Naples gave birth to the pizza in the mid-eighteenth century. Along with hotel and taxi, pizza is one of the few words understood worldwide.

Italy has more hotel rooms than any other nation.

Forty million tourists visit Italy per year. Tourism provides 63 per cent of the national income and it is the fourth most visited country in the world.

The language of music is Italian. The word 'scale' comes from the Italian word scala, meaning 'step.'

A thousand people an hour pass by Rome's Trevi Fountain. In the tourist season, €3,000 a day gets tossed into the fountain as people make a wish. The tradition of throwing a coin over your shoulder into the fountain is supposed to bring good luck and ensure a return to the Eternal City. At night, the money is collected by a Catholic charity service that provides food for the needy.

Italy houses 60 per cent of the world's art treasures.

The Carabinieri uniform was designed by fashion

designer Valentino.

There are forty-eight UNESCO World Heritage Sites registered in Italy, the most for a single country. Mount Etna in Sicily was the latest to be added in June 2013.

Venice has four hundred foot bridges.

There is an ancient Italian law that bans the cutting of hair on Mondays.

Football is the national sport. It was introduced into Italy by the English in the late 1800s. Italy has won the World Cup on four occasions. England has won it once.

Discover other books by Paul Wright on Amazon

The first book of the Italian trilogy is

An Italian Home - Settling by Lake Como

Just what is it like for a foreigner to live and work in a northern Italian village, and become part of the community? How tough is it to leave your home country and settle in a new one? What do you have to do to be accepted by the people who live in a village that has existed for over five hundred years? Award-winning mural and artist and stage designer Paul Wright and his partner Nicola found out the hard way, working, playing, laughing, eating and drinking alongside the residents of a beautiful lakeside village.

"Paul Wright's tribute to the robust pleasures of village life....brings out the generosity and humanity of the inhabitants of Lake Como"
Desmond O'Grady, Italian Insider Review

Available in Kindle and in paperback

Discover other books by Paul Wright on Amazon

The third book of the Italian trilogy is

Cats do eat Spaghetti
Living with our Rescue Cats

Paul Wright and his wife Nicola emigrated to Lake Como Italy in 1991. When, some years later they moved to a new apartment, where they found the square to which they had moved was occupied by a colony of feral cats, all of which were in poor condition. They began taking as many as they could to the vet's to be neutered, but soon adopted several. This story is dedicated to their twenty rescued cats and each one highlights the character of the individual, describing the pleasures and the sadness of a life that revolves around cats that will evoke sentiment and affection within the hearts of all committed cat lovers.

Available in Kindle and in paperback

Made in the USA
Las Vegas, NV
16 May 2021

23156463R00127